George Armatage

The horse

how to feed him, avoid disease, and save money

George Armatage

The horse
how to feed him, avoid disease, and save money

ISBN/EAN: 9783744739351

Printed in Europe, USA, Canada, Australia, Japan

Cover: Foto ©Lupo / pixelio.de

More available books at **www.hansebooks.com**

THE HORSE:

HOW TO FEED HIM, AVOID DISEASE,

AND SAVE MONEY.

BY

GEORGE ARMATAGE, M.R.C.V.S.,
PROFESSOR OF ANATOMY AND PHYSIOLOGY IN THE GLASGOW
VETERINARY COLLEGE;
LATE PROFESSOR OF MATERIA MEDICA, ETC., IN THE ALBERT VETERINARY
COLLEGE, ETC. ETC.

LONDON:
FREDERICK WARNE AND CO.
BEDFORD STREET, COVENT GARDEN.
1868.

INTRODUCTION.

In the preservation of our domestic animals, the capabilities and resources of Veterinary Science are too frequently ignored.

The question of feeding and housing is almost exclusively considered apart from the relationship which it bears to science. These have paved the way for absolute carelessness and quackery, and almost obliterated the aspect in which the practitioner of veterinary medicine should be regarded.

It is the province of the Veterinary Surgeon to study, not only the principles by which disease runs its course, its indications and cure; but also, and especially, those means by which it is primarily induced and *prevented.*

The means by which disease is prevented· have not hitherto been generally understood, nor have they been properly taught or studied in connection with the lower animals, hence the results in many individual cases have been manifest in utter ruin.

It is high time that they are thoroughly persevered in and encouraged, studied philosophically by the Veterinary Surgeon, and encouraged by the public, and suitable information disseminated in order to place those interested on the right road towards mitigating, if not producing a total immunity from, unnecessary evils and mortality.

It is a plan in which all owners of horses and other domestic animals are particularly interested, but are excusably ignorant.

Their attention cannot be directed to a profound study of those laws which are ever present, and govern the principles to be understood.

They require information and assistance, in order to apply it from time to time.

It is the province and duty of the Veterinary Surgeon to provide both, and I am convinced from experience that, were the disposition more frequently present, nothing would enhance so much the relations which exist between himself and employers, nor tend more to elevate our profession to that eminence which it deserves in the social economy.

The public is not such a short-sighted body as is generally supposed, and in watchfulness of its interests is ever ready to embrace those means by which an advance can be made. Neither is it such a selfish body, for when valuable information is ungrudgingly rendered, it quickly demonstrates its approbation, and the benefit derived is seldom allowed to pass without suitable acknowledgment and reward.

In an age of sensationalism, it is almost an

Introduction. vii

error to be otherwise than productive of startling fact or fiction.

The idea pervades more classes than one, and, it is to be feared, usefulness is thereby frequently neglected for the purely decorative. In many circles, the spirit crops out and displays the infection. Our limited professional arena forms no exception to the general condition of affairs, and demands our sympathy rather than censure.

I claim, however, to be useful in the following pages. The ornamental has been disregarded, while old matters are reproduced and presented under features which, it is hoped, will prove instructive and interesting.

In presenting this little treatise to the owners of horses, I am but carrying out the wishes of many excellent friends obtained throughout my professional career in various parts of England and Scotland. To them I cannot sufficiently express the obligations which are felt for the willingness with which I have been allowed to test the accuracy of my statements in regard to feeding, as a means of preventing disease, or otherwise, the immediate adoption by themselves of the principles which have been submitted.

Some with whom many hours of useful conversation on these topics have been held, are now no more—amongst them was foremost the Right Hon. the (fifth) Earl of Jersey—but their goodness still lives in memory as haloes of the past.

My thanks are especially due to W. Mirfin, Esq., Sheffield; to Richard Heckels, Esq., Monkwearmouth Colliery, and George Suthern, Esq., Hallgarth House, Durham. Also to Mr. Charles Hunting, M.R.C.V.S., South Hetton, Durham, and Mr. Luke Scott, M.R.C.V.S., Hetton, Durham, whose practical information, together with numerous opportunities afforded me to visit their horses and ponies below ground, have proved invaluable. There I have been enabled to witness the practical demonstration of that which they described, and farther testing the accuracy of observations previously made by myself.

To several gentlemen in Glasgow, particularly my colleagues and professional brethren, I am equally indebted, and thank them one and all.

It remains to be added, that the calculations as to cost of feeding have been placed in contrast in order to show that, although prices may fluctuate, and even rise considerably, by a judicious selection of grain and leguminous seeds the same amount of nitrogenous or nutritious matter may be supplied, and that too, at the same cost, or thereabouts.

English weights and measures are adhered to throughout.

VETERINARY COLLEGE,
 PARLIAMENTARY ROAD, GLASGOW.
  28*th February*, 1868.

CONTENTS.

	PAGE
INTRODUCTION.	V

PART I.

MISMANAGEMENT. 1

DEVELOPMENT AND MAINTENANCE:
Immediate Object of Food—Development—Maintenance—Waste or Decay—Importance of Good Food for Young Animals—Evils of an Insufficiency 8

ORGANS OF DIGESTION:
Enumeration—Prehension—Incisor Teeth—Tongue—Cheeks—Molars or Grinders—Pharynx—Gullet—Deglutition 14

INSALIVATION:
Saliva — Salivary Glands — Solvent Action — Chemical Action—Quantity of Saliva—Uses and Importance of Saliva 16

STOMACH:
Peculiarities in the Horse, Ox, and Man—Broken Wind, and Chronic Cough—Rapid Digestion in the Horse — Small Stomach — Necessity for Regular Feeding 20

INTESTINES:

Enumeration and Division—Length—Small Intestines — Digestion in—Secretions — Chyle—Lacteals—Absorption and Assimilation—Capacity—Large Intestines—Division—Absorption —Capacity 23

THE DIGESTIVE PROCESS:

A Complex Action — Gastric Digestion—Gastric Juice—Intestinal Digestion—Chyle—Formation of Blood 26

ELEMENTARY PRINCIPLES OF FOOD:

Enumeration—Flesh Formers—Heat Producers— Salts—Acids—Fæces or Dung 28

ESSENTIAL CHARACTERS OF FOOD:

Nutritious Principles—Their Identity from all Sources — Non-nutritious Principles — Animal Heat—Necessity for Substances of a Mixed Character—Bulk or Volume 29

ERRORS TO BE AVOIDED:

Fluids—Cooked Food—Injurious Effect of Common Salt—Diabetes and Albuminuria—Farcy and Glanders 40

ADVANTAGES OF PROPER FOOD AND SYSTEM . . . 46

REGULAR FEEDING 50

CALCULI OR STONES:

Their Origin—Different Kinds—Frequently Prove Fatal 51

OBJECTIONS TO THE USE OF DRY FOOD:

Do Oats Pass Out Unchanged?—Proofs—Necessity for Healthy Condition—Care Required in Feeding —Importance of a Superintendent 54

PART II.

VARIETIES OF FOOD:
Nutrition in Each — Maize — Oats — Cost of Feeding Upon—Measure and Weight should be Combined 63

SELECTION AND PURCHASE OF GRAIN 68

ECONOMY OF FOOD:
Indian Corn Injurious—Linseed—Tares—Mixtures Necessary 70

SYSTEMS ADOPTED ON VARIOUS COLLIERIES:
Hunting on Cut Food—Hetton System 74

WHAT CONSTITUTES A CHEAP FOOD 81

OBJECTIONS TO A CHANGE OF GRAIN 82

BEAN, ITS NATURE, USES, AND ABUSES 83

LONDONDERRY COLLIERY SYSTEM:
Mixture—Steamed Food—Waste, &c. 85

FORMS OF ADMIXTURE:
Low Rates—High Rates 89

GREEN FOOD, ITS BENEFIT AND INJURY 97

ECONOMY IN USING CHAFF AND BRUISED CORN . 99

PEA AND BEAN STRAW 101

SAVING TO BE EFFECTED. 102

IMPORTANCE OF GROOMING 104

THE HORSE.

PART I.

Mismanagement.

MISMANAGEMENT in any department is universally acknowledged to be the precursor of evil consequences, and one of the golden rules in our social economy is that which teaches how to recognise the one and avert the other.

If there is a section of the community which languidly basks in the oblivion of misrule more than another, it is that under whose care are placed our valuable domestic animals, and to which we trace deterioration of breed, prevalence of disease, and a high rate of mortality.

As things at present exist in the many places to which these remarks apply, one would be inclined to the opinion that the study of *system* in the stable and cow-shed is unworthy the time, trouble, attention, or altogether useless: hence the result; valuable animals are left to the care of illiterate attendants, who prescribe for their wants and comforts under predominate ignorance. At one time they are fed with extravagance, and at another a nutritious meal is denied them.

Unwarranted officiousness also too frequently provides a novel system, and wonders are speedily developed in adverse of a desirable state, while indisputable obstinacy and prejudice prevent the recognition of cause and effect.

In ignorance of the nature of food, principles of feeding and management, the annual losses from indigestion and its consequences among horses and cattle are somewhat startling, and unfortunately too common throughout Great Britain. Even in places where we have a right to expect practical information on the laws of health and the animal economy, confusion only remains. This is particularly the case upon some of the large colliery establishments in the north of England.

Immense numbers of horses and ponies are here fed in accordance with principles laid down by a "land agent," upon corn usually purchased by himself. These principles are generally original, and resemble the laws of the "Medes and Persians" in being unalterable.

During one part of the year, corn with an excess of green food is supplied; at another, the grain is spoiled by steaming; each period being regulated in total ignorance and disregard of existing conditions, *without instituting the least inquiry in most cases, and never making a descent of the mines* to examine the animals which come in for a share of such magnanimous solicitude.

Besides this functionary, there are other members of the executive called "viewers," who do not forget their exalted position, attained in some instances, I fear, at a speed which has not admitted of the mind assuming an adaptability to it; at least, judging from the amount of presumption with which these men vaunt their opinions upon professional matters, and in their want of respect to others infinitely higher in the social scale.

Under such principles of "grandeeism," it is not surprising that, with unsystematic feeding, hard work unnecessarily protracted, with cruelty overlooked or connived at, mortality is excessive. The ears of reason are, however, stopped, and as some one must bear blame when it is forthcoming, he who possesses the least influence in the matter —the resident veterinary surgeon—receives the whole in a most ignominious manner.

Happily all are not of this kind.

Some of my best friends are engaged in the management of extensive collieries, and have amply shown what can be done to ameliorate the life and condition of the poor creatures employed there. Such bear a remarkable contrast to the former class, who never recognise the efforts of others except when they can be appropriated as their own good deeds, by which they seek the adulation of the owner, and swamp into insignificance him who feels it an imperative duty to utter a word for reform or economy. This is the "red-tape," for the exercise of which

I presume owners who know it not pay rather dearly.

It has been known that reports detailing the existence of glaring evils easily remedied by a change of system, requiring no extra outlay, but insuring a highly profitable investment, drawn up by able men — veterinary surgeons—who have studied these matters for years and practised them successfully, and who, after sending them to headquarters by desire, have been treated contemptuously—such men have been told, "*your information is only a parcel of figures,*" or after being summoned to the office of the "viewer," "*you had better not interfere in such matters; things have gone along very well hitherto, and no complaint has been made from above; you receive your salary, and it will be advisable that you should not report these things beyond myself.*"

Existing affairs are permitted to go on as before, but the information thus obtained is put aside, in order to be applied as perfectly original matter at a time when the proper owner is not present to identify it.

A few years ago, in a paper read before a certain farmers' club, I gave the details of a system of feeding colliery horses which had been successfully carried on by the resident veterinary surgeon some years, and resulted in the annual saving of hundreds of pounds.

The local newspapers gave full reports, the executive was jealous of the honour given, and

Mismanagement.

immediately took the feeding into their own hands.

On another occasion Mr. Hunting, M.R.C.V.S., attended the Newcastle Farmers' Club, in obedience to a request, to detail the system which he had carried out successfully both as to the saving of expenditure and preventing mortality. The usual feeling of malice and jealousy prevailed here also, for some unknown person forwarded a parcel of hay-seeds and rubbish to the chairman, with the statement that the sample was taken from the kind of provender which Mr. Hunting used, and was about to recommend to the meeting.

Such is the treatment with which professional men are met upon some of the extensive colliery estates of Britain. Instructions received from "head-quarters" point out the necessity for surveillance over the provender, mode of feeding, work, &c., by the veterinary-surgeon; but to detect an error and point it out as required, although an enormous saving would accrue from a change, is to render him odious in the eyes of despotism. If he wishes to hold his appointment, it must be by the sacrifice of conscientious duty, an assumed blindness to, and perfect silence upon, such topics. If he persists in his course, the results are known only to himself.

While this treatment is permitted, it is not very likely that great improvements, or the avoidance of unnecessary expenditure, waste, and mortality will take place in the departments referred to. Owners may still complain about the disparity between profits and expenses. Efficient veterinary surgeons (and there are men in the body of practitioners as valuable in their calling as viewers are in theirs), desirous of establishing necessary and profitable reformation in departments *essentially their own*, lose interest, and weary in well-doing after repeated insults of the kind referred to are heaped upon them. They are not allowed a word in explanation, and at length retire in disgust, and the places are filled by automatons—mere machines—who generally occupy such posts with greater satisfaction to those who fill up the executive and revel in the exercise of despotic power.

It is not only in reference to colliery animals where mismanagement occurs. We need but turn our attention to the system pursued in our large town and farm stables; and cattle and sheep also are found to participate in the general results.

Veterinary surgeons in some districts can testify to the bulk of their cases being those which arise from indigestion, and the insurance papers of many a defunct society would afford doleful tales of sudden death from the same states, causing rupture of the stomach, intestines, or diaphragm, calculi (or stones), and incurable diabetes running into farcy and glanders.

Farmers are fully conversant with similar results also, which find an origin in the cheap

Mismanagement. 7

and inferior bean or pea straw, musty hay, and supposed economical system of feeding with little or no corn.

Among his cattle he endures losses from engorged and ruptured stomach, splenic apoplexy, black-leg, parturient diseases, diarrhœa, and dysentery; and among his sheep, in addition to the above, skin and parasitic diseases.

The London brewers have to lament the loss of their plump dray horses from rupture and disease of the liver; and Scotch proprietors suffer no less, though rather differently, from the use of trashy boiled mixtures of food.

In the coal mines, where proper surveillance is not permitted, and stupid customs are adhered to, indigestion, with its attendant states, carries off many valuable lives, and the cause is looked upon as inducing a condition which must be endured, or the evil as a manifestation of some peculiar influence, probably of a planetary character.

Notwithstanding this, all busy themselves in searching for a *cure*, without going further to attempt a solution of the mystery, which may be interpreted by the principle of *prevention*. We thus go on in blindness and obstinacy, seeking after some brilliant theory, and in eager pursuit of that which is remote, neglect the highly profitable and easily deciphered lessons which, already pregnant with most ample information, are completely within the grasp.

Development and Maintenance.

A discussion of the subject of food and its application to the animal fabric, involves a consideration of scientific principles which reveal the exact nature of the substances employed, their transformation within the organism, and the offices they perform at their destination.

The *immediate object of food* is the development and maintenance of the animal body.

Development may be briefly stated to be that process by which the various parts or organs assume their relative form, size, and capabilities for functional activity—*e.g.*, secretion, excretion, and the like. Development is principally referable to intra-uterine life, or that period during which the future animal lies within the womb of its mother, when the various organs, as the brain, heart, lungs, liver, and in fact all parts of the body, are acquiring their peculiar and characteristic form.

Each primitive portion gradually and constantly receives fresh additions, and each stage constitutes also a farther elaboration and assumption of higher powers.

Development continues also throughout a period after birth. The long-legged, weedy-looking foal is an example excellently suitable for the purpose of illustration. Although as far as internal organs are concerned, development may be said to be in a measure complete, yet there

Development and Maintenance.

are important changes to be otherwise effected. The muscles of the body are small and pale, and the bones (so called) are very deficient in osseous material (earthy salts). A few teeth only are through the gums, and others are lying in different stages beneath in the form of a highly vascular pulp, quite unlike its future self.

In each there are important changes to take place.

The bundles of cartilage in the centre of the limbs and beneath the muscles of the body, &c., gradually become harder, and lose their characteristic elasticity. Their structure is altered by the deposition of bony material, and by and bye we have the osseous framework or skeleton completed.

The pale muscular fibres assume greater dimensions, and at the same time a darker colour, and power to act more forcibly on the individual bones.

The tooth pulp within the gums, already provided with innumerable blood vessels and nerves, gradually acquires the shape of a tooth, incisor or molar, its different layers of hard substance variously termed dentine, enamel, &c., and only at a specified time will it appear above the surface.

At length the animal is "filled up," "made up," or "furnished," in stable phraseology, and the period of *youth* gives way to that which is known as the *adult stage*.

Maintenance has been going on throughout the whole of this time. Functional activity is attended by a process of *waste* or *decay* of the parts implicated. This process will be hereafter expressed as *metamorphosis of tissues*.

In no period of life can this process be said to be dormant or non-existent, but in none so slow or so little required as in early youth. At this time the building up of the animal body by the accumulation of blood, bone, muscle, hoof, horn, teeth, hair, &c., &c., is actively carried on, and their waste or decay comparatively small. In adult life, however, when development has gone on to completion, and great exertion is called forth, metamorphosis or change in the constitution of the tissues above mentioned is great.

This requires the process of maintenance or repair to restore, during repose, that which has being constantly lost during activity or exercise.

The movements of the arms or legs in walking, the tongue and jaws in speaking, lungs during respiration, heart in its beating, and intestines during contraction,—in short, any act, voluntary or involuntary, which calls forth muscular movements in any part of the animal body, is attended with the expenditure of vital force, as shown in the change or alteration of the condition, waste, decay, or metamorphosis of the composing material.

During metamorphosis of tissue chemical

Development and Maintenance. 11

action is instituted, and new compounds are produced which are no longer useful to the body. They are called *effete* materials, and after being collected by appropriate vessels termed *lymphatics*, are by them conveyed to special organs for the purpose of being expelled. If retained, they would prove highly detrimental to the body, and even destructive to life.

The *waste of muscular tissue* from work and ordinary exercise is considerable, that substance forming a great portion of the animal body. It is constantly in need of fresh material to restore or replace those parts which have been removed by waste, and the elements necessary are provided by the food, after undergoing important changes hereafter to be mentioned under digestion.

Such facts, briefly as they are detailed, and divested, as far as practicable, of technicalities, present most important points to view, and enable us to direct particular attention to the application and economising of material (food) for the production of the greatest amount of actual force—strength and vigour in working animals, or of fat in those destined for the butcher.

With these before us, the effects of some of the modes in which animals are kept, will be clearly understood.

Under the subject of development it has been stated the process is confined to intra-uterine

Development and Maintenance.

life and early periods of youth. It is then we find the great demands upon the system in order to complete the formation and building up of the whole body. Every one almost knows that much more food than ordinarily is consumed by the pregnant mare or cow, and that the young animal consumes much food of a nutritious quality without the appearance being in all cases obviously benefited thereby.

These illustrations serve to show the great demands for blood, bone, muscle, skin, hair, hoof, tendons, &c. &c., and a moment's reflection will cause one to pause and wonder how some persons can really expect to make a horse, cow, or other animal upon the quantities of miserable rubbish which are put in the poor creatures' way when young.

How they can witness their colts and calves standing without cover in an empty straw-yard or bare pasture in the cold and rain during the winter, and expect the grass of the coming summer will make up for the previous starvation, is indeed a paradox. It appears quite sufficient with some that a horse should taste corn only when he is able to earn it, and cattle when they commence to give milk, or there are prospects of their being useful to the butcher.

All this is mistaken policy. The young horse or ox requires ample food for the building up of the frame, and we discern the wise provision of nature in furnishing the rich elements in the

Development and Maintenance. 13

milk of the mother. Both need highly nutritious food, and when this is denied, the owner finds he is on the sure road towards spoiling them. They always suffer acutely when good food is afterwards given; the change serves only to engender serious, if not fatal, disease. Instances will be found in the maladies *black-leg* or *quarter-evil, splenic apoplexy, blain*, &c., of cattle and sheep.

In the horse we find, when put to work for the first time, he is "unable to stand the corn;" the legs swell, coat stares, he performs his work badly, and there are other indications of a disordered state within.

Colic, or *purpura hæmorrhagica*, speedily kills him, or he is left to dole out a miserable existence with protracted suffering from *chronic disease of the lungs* or *liver, diabetes, canker, laminitis* (founder), constant attacks of *lymphangitis* (weed), and *farcy*, terminating, after effectually propagating the contagion, in *glanders* and *death*.

As life and development proceeds, food then serves a different purpose. While it is expended in supplying fresh elements to the blood, that fluid has now to furnish elaborate materials to replace the constituents of the body lost during waste of muscle and other tissues, which are rendered visible in the shape of the products of respiration, perspiration, the urine, and fæces. What formerly went to form muscle, bone, &c., now goes to repair them. The blood in all cases is the fluid which furnishes the *pabulum* whence tissues derive their support. That fluid is maintained by regular additions of elements obtained from the food. The process which prepares them we have to consider shortly.

Organs of Digestion.

The organs of digestion comprise the *mouth, teeth, tongue, salivary glands, pharynx, œsophagus* or *gullet, stomach, intestines, liver*, and *pancreas* or *sweetbread*.

In connexion with the mouth we find appropriate muscles forming the bulk of the lips and sides for the *prehension* or gathering of food, and *incisor teeth* or *nippers*—six above and below in the horse, and six only below in the ox, sheep, deer, &c.—for the purpose of cutting off the herbage. Within the mouth the *tongue* performs the important office of distinguishing by the peculiar sense of taste, the difference in each variety of substances introduced, and moves them from side to side in order to bring them within the pressure of the *molar teeth* or *grinders*. The *tongue* at length, by a contraction upon itself backwards, carries the bolus of food with it, which is then seized by the pharynx, and passes immediately along the gullet to the stomach.

The *cheeks* on each side being formed of

Organs of Digestion. 15

muscles, assist materially in keeping the food effectually between the molar teeth. Through their substance pass ducts or tubes which convey necessary lubricating and solvent fluids to the mouth.

The *molars* or *grinders* are twenty-four in number, six of which are situated above and below upon each side of the jaws in the back part of the mouth. In order to observe them particularly the mouth must be held wide open.

They are large and rough upon the wearing surface, and form most perfect agents in crushing and grinding, or masticating the hard grain and kernels which this animal requires as natural food.

The *pharynx* is a musculo-membranous bag or pouch which opens at the back of the mouth, and grasps the bolus of food as it is presented by the tongue. Arrived at this point, its appropriate muscles successively contract and force onwards the pellet to the further end opening into the gullet. The food is now beyond the control of the will, and cannot be returned by any effort of a natural character.

The *œsophagus* or *gullet* is also composed partly of muscles and membrane. It forms an elastic tube reaching from the pharynx above to the stomach below, and occupies a position in the neck upon the left side of the lower portion. A knowledge of this fact enables us to trace the passage of substances throughout its visible course. The remaining part of the gullet passes through the chest, and is called the *thoracic* portion. The passage of food through the pharynx and gullet is termed *deglutition* or swallowing.

Insalivation.

The mouth is abundantly supplied with fluid for the purpose of lubricating its surfaces during motion in mastication. It also possesses peculiar solvent and chemical actions upon alimentary matters introduced, and thus effects special changes in their constitution, of vital importance to digestion and assimilation.

Saliva is the name given to this fluid, and is the produce of glands in the vicinity, the largest, the parotid gland, being placed below the ear behind the angle of the lower jaw. In addition there are others of a smaller character situated beneath the tongue, between the sides of the jaw, inside the lips and other parts; all of which separately contribute important properties to the fluids which mix in the mouth, whence they are conveyed by appropriate tubes or ducts.

The *solvent action* of *saliva* depends upon the presence of peculiar salts and a principle called *ptyalin* by scientific men, and is easily demonstrated by placing food within the mouth. It is also found to act efficiently when collected in suitable vessels and brought into contact with

Insalivation. 17

certain alimentary matters. Its power of altering the constitution of compounds is purely a *chemical action*, and is most peculiarly well marked upon those of a starchy character, abundance of which are found in the food upon which horses and cattle subsist. Through this influence they are converted into a principle called *dextrine*, and subsequently into *grape sugar*.

The salivary glands are under the control of the nervous system. In the human subject, the sight or smell of food of an agreeable character is sufficient to cause a copious flow to the mouth; hence the common expression " the mouth waters."

Saliva is secreted abundantly. The exact amount of this fluid which is formed is not easily obtained. A large horse is supposed to secrete 84lbs. per day, an ox 102lbs. Mr. Hunting obtained half a gallon, or about five pounds in half an hour.

The *uses of saliva* are important and manifold. First, we have an abundant flow; second, its peculiar solvent power; third, its chemical action in converting starchy matters into sugar; fourth, its lubricating qualities during the presence of absorbing, or coarse and rough, substances; fifth, *it is secreted in major part during mastication, and continues as long as that act is carried on.*

This category of properties in a simple-looking fluid like saliva must have been conferred for a beneficial purpose.

c

Insalivation.

We find such to be a law throughout nature. That purpose is essentially the primary step in rendering the component parts of the food assimilable, *i.e.*, converting them into constituent parts of the blood.

Being secreted at the time when the food is undergoing comminution between the teeth, it is presented at a period when it will be most effective. Food, therefore, which is swallowed quickly or greedily, without proper mastication, obtains little saliva, and the necessary transformations are not carried out.

It is impossible to supply a fluid artificially which can take the place of saliva. Mere saturation of the food by water does not promote digestibility as a consequence.

This has been satisfactorily proved many times. If the salivary glands are prevented from discharging their contents into the mouth during mastication, and water is thrown among the mass within the stomach, digestion is retarded. We have positive evidence of this in daily practice in those establishments where owners persist in using boiled mixtures of food, which is done in utter neglect of the most important fact that the horse has perfect grinders to crush and break down everything which comes in the way of *natural* food, with the best solvent immediately at hand, and in unlimited quantity, to effect a primary transformation towards the production of blood, bone, muscle, hoof, hair, &c. &c.

Insalivation.

The practice is an attempt to set aside nature, and might be excused if none of the above appliances are present, or their capabilities in part destroyed. We are so accustomed to treat the horse by analogy, thus convicting him in the exercise of irregular practices, errors of body and mind in common with ourselves, that we naturally prescribed a mode of treatment based upon conditions supposed to exist.

Even a moderate acquaintance with the organized fabric of man and the higher animals leads to a different conclusion. It proves the practice unscientific, unsystematic, foreign, and *unnatural*.

I shall have more to offer upon the question of boiled food when a description of other organs has been given.

After the food has undergone the necessary processes of mastication and insalivation, and, as it passes backwards in the act of swallowing or *deglutition*, it becomes coated with a thick mucous or viscous secretion, thrown out from glands on the inner surface of the pharynx and gullet. It accumulates as the mass descends, and forms a thick greasy kind of coating, the proceeding having for its object mainly the avoidance of aggregation and stoppage in the gullet, a condition which under aggravated states constitutes choking.*

---

* It not uncommonly happens after hard work and long fasts the horse, returning weary and hungry, ravenously swallows his

The Stomach.

Descending the gullet the bolus of food at length reaches the stomach, a pouch or dilatation of that tube. In the stomach further important changes are executed in the constitution of the food.

In man this organ performs the greater portion of the process of digestion. In the horse and ox but little analogy exists, and the essential points of difference will repay even a cursory examination.

The ox is endowed with four stomachs, or what is more in keeping with anatomical description, a quadrisect stomach, *i.e.*, containing four distinct compartments, each of which possesses different functions.

The first compartment is one of immense capacity. It occupies three-fourths of the abdomen, and is able to accommodate a great quantity of ingesta.

The second is small, and contains more fluid

---

food without due mastication and insalivation. The secretions are deficient by reason of fatigue or nervous depression and other causes. The bolus is speedily despatched, almost dry, and choking is apt to occur in its worst forms. If the food reaches the stomach aggravated colic is almost certain.

See my Prize Essay "On the Diseases of Farm Horses," published in the Transactions of the Highland and Agricultural Society of Scotland, Article—" Choking."

The Stomach.

than the first, but both act in common in macerating and securing successive changes in the food.

The third exerts a degree of pressure, by means of its peculiar leaves, upon the alimentary matters arrested by it.

The fourth is the true digestive compartment, and resembles the stomach of man and the dog principally.

The ox is essentially an animal capable only of limited and not rapid exertion. The structure and arrangement of the digestive organs are clearly intended to accommodate large quantities of herbage of a mixed character, for which the functions are admirably fitted.

The horse, on the other hand, being made and required for rapid exertion, could not fulfil those ends with the digestive organs of the ox, and, therefore, like man and the carnivora, but one stomach or compartment is provided, which is both comparatively and relatively smaller.

The process of digestion is also wonderfully effective.

Whilst the ox has been known to retain food for upwards of six weeks within his stomach, little more than as many hours will suffice to ensure digestion in the horse. The process is, therefore, also wonderfully rapid.

The stomach of the horse, replete with food, acts as a great impediment to the action of the lungs, hence the great number of cases of *broken wind* and *chronic cough*, which are known to occur from irregular principles of feeding.

The horse cannot occupy himself in rumination or digestion almost entirely as the ox. He is required to undertake the removal of heavy loads, or otherwise engaged in rapid exertion. A rapid digestion in his stomach is therefore a very wise provision to relieve the lungs during action.

I have purposely exhibited substances of different degrees of solubility, and possessing a strong odour, to animals about to be slaughtered, and have been particularly struck with the fact that, in the short space of time which has elapsed between the administration of the medicine and opening the stomach, not a trace beyond the odour of the substance could be detected. The paper in which it was wrapped was usually found in the stomach, but the medicine had passed several yards along the gut, frequently within one hour.

Similar facts are observable with regard to food. I have known horses and ponies suddenly killed in coal mines by a fall of portions of the roof within one or two hours after a meal, and on examining the stomach it has been observed that digestion has progressed rapidly and effectively in that organ, only a small portion, the most indigestible, remaining behind. The more easily digestible portion had usually passed along the intestines in distances varying from ten to twenty feet or more.

The Intestines. 23

It is a rule that all portions of greater solubility in the secretions, *i.e.*, more digestible, first pass out from the stomach in health.

Fluids also pass rapidly. They are usually carried to the cæcum, a large gut situate about twenty yards from the stomach in large horses, twenty minutes being usually sufficient.

These illustrations definitely explain why a horse occupies so much time consuming food. Put him into the stable after a day's work, and he will be found eating the greater part of the night. A small stomach, capable of effective and rapid action, is quickly emptied of its contents, and the desire for food, therefore, becomes almost constant.

We should gather from this also the absolute necessity of a regular supply of food, and abolition of long fasts and full racks and mangers when the animal returns to the stable.

The Intestines.

The intestines are of two kinds, small and large. In the horse they occupy the greater portion of the cavity of the abdomen, and constitute the largest part of the alimentary track.

The whole length may be estimated at about ninety feet, or ranging from twenty-six to thirty yards.

The *small intestines* commence at the stomach, and in their course receive the several names, *duodenum, jejunum,* and *ilium,* the divisions being purely imaginary.

About five or six inches below the stomach are the orifices which discharge the secretions of the liver (bile) and pancreas (a fluid resembling saliva). Besides these, other special fluids are poured from the walls (coats) throughout the length of the canal.

The walls are strong and provided with muscular fibres, as the gullet and stomach, to produce the necessary contractions (vermicular or worm-like) in order to subject the contents (ingesta) to the action of the various fluids, as well as cause it to pass onwards.

Throughout the inner surfaces of the small intestines a number of peculiar vessels are seen to enter. Their office is to abstract the nutritious elements of the food, which after meeting with the various secretions in the tube, assumes a whitish creamy consistence, and is termed *chyle*. The vessels here spoken of are termed *lacteals*. They communicate with other vessels and glands. In them the chyle as it passes onwards alters its constitution, and by successive stages assumes the character of the blood with which it is afterwards mixed. This constitutes the process of *assimilation*.

The small intestines are from fifty to sixty feet in length, and will accommodate from eight to elevens gallons of fluid.

The Intestines. 25

The *large intestines* of the horse are very capacious organs. The first, the *cæcum*, is a large conical pouch or bag, usually known as the *blind gut*. In it are collected principally the fluids drank, together with solid matters. The former occupy the extremity, the latter remain at the base. Absorption of fluids takes place from the cæcum in large proportion, and its contents are usually alkaline from the changes which take place in starchy constituents.

The *colon* is continued next in order to the cæcum. It is doubled upon itself, both parts throughout its entire length being united by intervening tissue, and traverses both sides and front of the abdomen twice, terminating in the rectum near the point from which it arises from the cæcum on the right side.

The cæcum and colon do not possess such thick muscular walls as the small intestines, but strong bands run longitudinally on four sides. These being considerably shorter than the intestines, have the effect of drawing them into puckers or folds, forming on the inner side a number of pouches, which assist in giving the characteristic form to the fæces or dung in the horse.

The *rectum* is very strong and muscular, but not so capacious, tolerably cylindrical, and terminates the alimentary track at the *anus* or fundament. Absorption from the large intestines is principally confined to the cæcum. The colon and rectum minister but little to that process. The *capacity of the large intestines* greatly exceeds that of the small. The cæcum will contain about four gallons of fluid, the colon about twelve, and the rectum about three gallons.

The Digestive Process.

The process of digestion is most complex and important, and deservedly receives an extended notice in all authentic works on animal physiology. It is impossible here to do more than briefly notice the leading stages, which are indispensable, but sufficient towards explaining generally the object for which these pages are written.

Gastric digestion.—In the stomach the food, already incorporated with the salivary and other secretions, is subjected to peculiar movements or contractions of the muscular walls, described usually as a "churning action." It is thus moved from one part to another and further incorporated with secretions (gastric juice) derived from glands (gastric glands) situate in the walls of the organ.

The *gastric juice* possesses acid properties, and a peculiar principle termed *pepsine*, which with the action of the stomach effects a reduction of the food to a uniform mass. The particles are in a fine state of division, and albuminous prin-

The Digestive Process. 27

ciples chiefly suffer chemical decomposition. At length the whole becomes a thick fluid and passes through the *pyloric* orifice of the stomach to the small intestines.

This fluid is called *chyme*. It contains nutritious matters in a state of mechanical suspension, others in chemical and simple solution, while a third variety are unacted upon from various causes.

Chyme proceeds along the intestines by virtue of the peculiar action of the organs. It first meets with fluids from special glands in the vicinity of the outlet from the stomach. Next with those from the liver and pancreas (sweetbread). By constant motion perfect incorporation is effected, and the following outline of changes may be observed.

1st. The acid character of chyme is neutralized—it is now alkaline.

2nd. Albuminous matters escaping from the stomach unchanged are transformed.

3rd. Starchy matters, unacted upon by saliva, are now effectually converted into sugar.

4th. Fatty bodies are emulsified or converted into a kind of soap.

5th. and lastly, all the nutritious principles have conferred upon them properties which facilitate their absorption and passage through the lacteals towards the blood, and the fluid mass now receives the name of *chyle*.

Chyle passes through the lacteals from the intestines. Its constituents gradually form a granular-looking mass, in which float a number of small vesicles or cells. By passage through an assemblage of bodies called *mesenteric glands*, the cells increase in number, and at length acquire colour, and eventually are poured into blood vessels near the heart. It is thus the blood becomes the pabulum whence all tissues are nourished. In the elements of food are found the materials which, after assimilation, partake of the characters of the tissues of the body; and the circulation of the blood explains how each kind receives its share.

Elementary Principles of Food.

The chyle contains the whole of the elements of the food. These are of a mixed character. First, we have *nitrogenous*, so-called because they contain largely the gas nitrogen, or *albuminous* principles which are strictly the elements from which muscle is developed—hence the term "flesh formers" which is applied to them. Second, we have *fatty bodies* and *saccharine* or sugary principles—starch, gum, sugar, &c.—*heat-producers*. Third, there are essential constituents in the form of *salts*—of lime, potash, soda, magnesia, &c. Fourth, various *acids*, as hydrochloric (muriatic acid or spirits of salt), nitric (aquafortis), sulphuric (oil of vitriol), lactic and phosphoric, &c.

In a chemical point of view the acids are most powerful agents, and by union with various substances form compounds of vital importance.

Lastly, there are compounds of no service whatever to the system. These are principally indigestible bodies, such as ligneous or fibrous parts of plants and foreign bodies which have gained access to the digestive organs, cells, earthy matter, and portions of undigested food which have been present in excess. Liebig has termed these the incombustible and unburned parts of food. They are the refuse from the digestive process, and together with *effete* or useless parts thrown off from the system, constitute the *fæces* or *dung*.

Essential Characters of Food.

Certain conditions are essential for the proper digestion and assimilation of food. When properly understood, they indicate the principles of an economical system of feeding animals with a view towards the preservation of health and vigour under continued laborious exertion, as well as preventing an undue rate of mortality resulting from it, and at a low rate of cost.

These conditions are, first, that food should be nutritious; second, that it contains elements of a mixed character; third, that it possesses proportionate bulk; fourth, it should be regularly supplied; and lastly, the digestive organs generally must be in a state of healthy action.

It is imperative that food possess *nutritious principles*. This must be apparent from the fact that from it all parts of the body are built up and being constantly renovated. In order to possess this property, bodies rich in nitrogen are requisite, which are denominated *nitrogenous, azotised, nutritious,* or *flesh-forming compounds*. Examples of these are *albumen, fibrine,* and *caseine*—terms which would indicate different substances. Chemically, however, they are alike in composition, but exhibit physically different appearances.

If wheaten flour be placed under a stream of cold water a sticky paste is left behind. This is called *gluten,* and is identical in chemical composition with the flesh of man and animals. It is the nitrogenous or albuminous principle of wheat flour.

If an egg be broken a glairy fluid escapes from the shell, which becomes white and coagulates into a solid mass when heated. This is *albumen* —gluten in another form, identical in composition, and is the nitrogenous principle of the egg from which the flesh, feathers, claws, &c., of the bird are formed.

If milk is taken and an acid added, a solid mass of curds is speedily produced. This is

Essential Characters of Food. 31

caseine—or gluten, albumen, and fibrine in another form, supplied in the milk of the mother to young animals, and in peas, beans, &c., to older ones; from which also hoof, horn, hair, wool, skin, flesh, and feathers, &c. &c., are formed, developed, and repaired.

Lastly, if blood be coagulated, the mass which separates proves itself an identical compound to flesh itself—*fibrine*.

The whole then are the various forms in which the elements are conveyed to the blood, as found in the food upon which the animal subsists. By the action of vital processes within the system, each assumes those conditions which in themselves are vital. Their supply to the system must be constant in order to keep pace with the waste. Hence they are found abundantly in the food upon which man and animals live. Horses and cattle meet with them in the grass and corn which they daily consume, and man and carnivora obtain it directly by using the flesh and blood (fibrine) of animals as food.

The following table shows how these substances resemble each other in chemical composition :—

	Gluten from flour. Boussingault.	Caseine from peas. Scherer.	Albumen from eggs. Jones.	Ox-blood. Playfair.	Ox-flesh. Playfair.
Carbon	54·2	54·138	55·000	54·35	54·12
Hydrogen	7·5	7·156	7·073	7·50	7·89
Nitrogen	13·9	15·672	15·920	15·76	15·67
Oxygen	24·4	23·034	22·007	22·39	22·32
	100·0	100·000	100·000	100·000	100·000

Non-nutritious Principles.

In addition to the flesh-forming constituents of food, there are also needed others known as *non-nitrogenous, non-azotised*, or *non-nutritious*, so named in contradistinction to those which contain nitrogen. Examples are found in starch, sugar, gum, and fat itself. They are composed of carbon, hydrogen, and oxygen, *minus* nitrogen, and are found abundantly in the different varieties of corn and vegetables used as food.

Their services are required in the system equally with the albuminous compounds, but for a different purpose, *viz.*, the production of animal heat, and formation and storing up of fat within the system.

Animal Heat.

In order to render somewhat intelligible the principles upon which heat is developed, and maintained in the body, and the part which food plays in that process, attention must again be directed to facts.

Here it must be understood that although the term "heat producer" is applied to the saccharine principles of food, it by no means establishes an isolated fact. They are *not* the sole agents in the production of animal heat. I will attempt to explain.

Animal Heat.   33

To those who have studied chemistry, even but a little, the rapid development of heat unbearable in water previously cold is familiar. It is a good illustration for our purpose.

A quantity of cold water is taken in a tumbler or other thin glass vessel, and held in the hand, taking care to grasp that part in contact with the water. Sulphuric acid (oil of vitriol) is then added in nearly equal quantity, when by chemical action, which immediately takes place between the acid and water, intense heat is developed, rendering it an impossibility to hold the vessel in the manner adopted at the commencement.

The rubbing together of certain substances, or beating of metals upon hard surfaces, also produces great heat. Here the molecular disturbance—or the alteration of position of the ultimate particles composing the mass—which ensues from the concussion may not be unlike that which accompanies chemical action, although the means adopted to bring about each may be different.

It is, however, an undoubted fact that heat is developed by the chemical union of substances outside the body, and similar conditions are now found to apply to substances which are contained within it.

There are always met with elements and substances which, in contact with vital organs and their secretions assume the power of union by chemical action. They pervade the whole of the

D

tissues of the body. All the actions essential to life are carried on at the expense of the materials introduced, and those which are present as ready formed tissue. Their formation and development are attended with the union and disunion of the elements of compounds present, and their waste or decay is likewise attended with the same results. Thus we have a general chemical action, and this accounts for the equal state of temperature throughout the body.

Under ordinary circumstances the saccharine principles of food are being constantly caused to assume the form of fat, which under passive states, or where little exertion is carried on, is stored up beneath the skin, between muscles and around various organs, giving the animal that appearance of rotundity so much prized when intended for the butcher.

If an animal in such a condition were caused to exert himself for any length of time, the fat is absorbed and consumed. Its consumption is an essential act, not only in maintaining animal heat for the purposes of warmth, but as an agent which facilitates the decomposition of other bodies intended for the use of the system, in a different manner. Such an animal becomes lean. His muscles are distinctly observed to be well mapped out beneath the skin. The same appearance is also brought out by illness or disorder, and is the process generally understood as "wasting of the body."

Animal Heat.

There are a number of animals, as the hedgehog, (hybernating,) which during the summer become enormously fat, and sleep throughout the whole of the winter. In this case, as no food is taken, the body maintains its animal heat entirely by the consumption of fat which has been stored up in the system.

The bear also disposes of himself nearly in the same manner. It is also a notable fact that our cattle lay on, during the summer, a great quantity of fat, which is derived from the plentiful herbage of the period. In both these instances we also perceive the provision which is ensured towards obtaining the necessary amount of warmth during cold weather, and when food is either withheld or not very abundant.

Animal heat is not maintained by saccharine bodies or fat alone. In carnivorous animals, as the lion, tiger and wolf, whose diet is confined to flesh, also the wild hunters of some countries who occupy their time chiefly in the saddle, sufficient fat cannot be obtained, nor are saccharine compounds forthcoming. Natural warmth then must be procured from another source.

Wild animals in their natural state, and the hunters of uncivilised nations, are on an equality. The habits of both necessitate much exertion—activity of muscle—and consequently waste or decay.

Flesh, upon which they live, being purely a nitrogenous compound, would furnish none of the materials for warmth under other circumstances. But under active work or movements, albuminous compounds are broken up, and the carbonaceous elements rendered available for the purpose.

A reference to the table at page 31 will explain how this can be permitted. In farther explanation it may be stated, that fatty or saccharine compounds are serviceable *only* for the production of heat as an adjunct to vital force; but nitrogenous compounds are capable, by peculiar action, of becoming not only useful for the manufacture of flesh, but also for the production of the necessary animal heat during exercise or work.

This explains why animals in high condition appear fresh and excited. There is a necessity for movement created in order to consume the highly nutritious material within the body. Wild animals confined to cages are seen to move about incessantly when awake. Here is another mode in which the system endeavours to appropriate the food, and bring about essential vital actions. Were it not thus, disease or death would be an early result, from an accumulation of deleterious principles in the blood, by which it is no longer able to support the body.

Man and animals consume little food when the body is covered by fat, and exercise but sparingly taken. The muscles are not developed because they are not used, in fact such a body is not capable of much exertion, by reason of that want of muscular development. It is neither so healthy, and is prone to disease in consequence of the absence of movements which promote vital action.

These facts are well known to practical horse owners, and they in consequence always avoid fat animals for immediate active work, and delay until the place is occupied by muscle.

We thus perceive that in feeding fatting animals and working horses two opposite principles must be carried out. It would be as absurd to feed a hunter or draught horse on the materials given to the cow or ox in the feeding house, as to expect they should replace each other in the scale of usefulness to man.

These facts dispose of the first and second propositions. We find that food is nutritious when it can minister to the formation and development of the body, and maintenance against waste; while substances of a mixed character are needed in order to keep pace with the requirements of the body in the production of a necessary temperature, and assistance in the accumulation of vital force.

Without materials specially provided for the latter process our working animals would be reduced to the condition of flesh-eating or caged wild creatures, with this serious disadvantage, the work imposed might act prejudicially, as it would not, in all cases, be so nicely proportioned as to suit the wants of the system, or when taken in accordance with the promptings of instinct in the creature itself. In short, food possessing elements exclusively of one kind, too rich in nitrogen, or too rich in carbon, at once proves insufficient to support life in a proper manner for any length of time. The experiments of Majendie and others who fed animals exclusively on one of the substances known as sugar, gum, starch, albumen, fibrine, or caseine, set this matter at rest for ever, and we are thereby taught that the animal economy can live and thrive only upon food provided *naturally*, and which contains *all* the elements calculated to minister to the tissues and functions of the body.

The poor inhabitants of Ireland, as well as the negroes of the Indies, also establish the truth of the principle. The former, who consume potatoes in large quantity, would exist in a poor degree of capability for exertion, were they not to add to this expensive and innutritious article of diet one of the compounds very rich in nitrogen, *viz.*, milk.

The coolies, who eat impure sugar, receive with it also nitrogenous compounds, gathered from the vegetable kingdom, and all the eaters of maize and rice resort to milk for the azotised principle, caseine.

Food, rich in mixed characters, supplies the necessary elements without disturbing the balance of the functions, which occurs when too much of one kind is given indiscriminately. All vegetable food is of a mixed character, but each kind differs in the richness of its constituents. A

Bulk or Volume.

knowledge of this is of great value to all concerned in the keeping of animals.

Bulk or Volume.

Food should always possess an amount of bulk. Nature has not been unmindful of this when providing the nutritious principles of grain. The grain, or kernel, contains the nutrition in a concentrated form, and bulky material is to be found in the husk or stem.

Proportionate bulk is requisite to ensure digestion. The stomach cannot abstract nutrition from small quantities of concentrated food with benefit. The digestion and solution is not efficiently performed, as the stomach lacks the stimulus of contact, so essential to healthy action and secretion.

Grass, straw, and hay contain but little nutrition, and to ensure its abstraction, bulk is given to it consisting of water, ligneous matter (woody fibre), and salts.

The people of uncivilised nations have exemplified this from time remote.

The Kamschatdales mix earth and sawdust with the train oil they use as food, and in other northern regions a kind of bread is made from sawdust.

The natives of Ceylon use scraps of decayed wood with the honey consumed as food. Among animals the wolf is known to appease the sensations of hunger by taking into the stomach a great quantity of mud; the dog thrives best when he obtains his food from the ground, when it is mixed with grit and dirt, and in birds, small stones or sand is constantly being swallowed.

Food thus accompanied is fully compressed by the walls of the stomach, but when adventitious matters are not present, however nutritive, it does not fulfil the wants of the economy by virtue of its elements not being extracted.

Errors to be Avoided.

One of the great evils attendant upon the feeding of horses, and even cattle, is the use of *too bulky material*. By it the wants of the system are not satisfied, the stomach is over distended, and the process of chymifaction is retarded by the powers of the stomach being destroyed.

The walls are reduced in thickness, and rupture frequently takes place from the effects.

Fluids, however nutritious, as a rule, are not so easily appropriated as solid food. No better evidence is found than where cooked food is served to horses. The soft watery mass is too rapidly swallowed, and becomes as unnatural as it is innutritious.

It is an acknowledged fact that no process of cooking or preparation will render the food more

Errors to be Avoided. 41

nutritious, and there is positive proof that a mixture of substances, boiled to a pulp, are not so digestible as when given in a natural condition to working horses.

I do not expect that all who read this statement will be converted to the truth it proclaims. I am, however, certain that in the many places where the cooked system is carried out, there will be found persons desirous of successful reform and amelioration. To such I have great pleasure in addressing these pages. Others there are whom no amount of argument would convince, or practical demonstration convert. Bigotry, prejudice, and a stupid adherence to old customs have blinded them.

To change is considered unmanly, and, as existing affairs have probably prevailed for many years, unguided by either the light of reason or science, and having tradition only for their adoption and continuance, alterations would amount to sacrilege or disrespect to the blundering system which is worshipped with such folly and stupidity.

To resume. The stomach and intestines of the horse are not intended for sloppy food. The whole arrangement forms an assemblage of perfect organs eminently fitted for bruising, insalivating, digesting, and appropriating *natural* food, and unnatural slops and trash concocted by the device of man is attended with disease and mortality. Among horses, if we go no further than colic alone, the number of cases which occur where boiled food is used exceed those where attention is paid to the selection and supply of proper diet by *ninety per cent.*

Cooked food is open to grave objections. It weakens the digestive organs. It is swallowed rapidly, and the stomach becomes greatly distended, by which secretions are prevented or altogether stopped. Little or no insalivation takes place, and the food does not undergo those important and preliminary changes which have already been insisted upon. Secretions, otherwise necessary, are of no use with such an excess of fluid food, and if poured out are too far diluted. The stomach acquires in time an immense capacity and the muscular powers are weakened. The liver becomes diseased and the natural secretions very limited or absent. The intestines now suffer from this combination of results, and colic becomes of periodical occurrence, eventually ending in death.

The horses of many firms with which I am acquainted in Scotland, to whom boiled food is given, suffer very frequently from colic, and deaths are common.

Where proper systems are carried out, I have known three hundred animals belonging to one firm, doing the hardest work, kept in the best of health, and for a whole year not a single case occurs.

Mr. Hunting states that 120 pit animals under

Errors to be Avoided. 43

his care, all in regular work, continued for six years without a single case of colic.

The bulk given to boiled food is looked upon by some as an advantage, and in illustration of the belief, a gentleman remarked recently that the food thus supplied to his horses must be more nutritious than other kinds, as it is softer, partially digested to begin with, and every twelve pounds put into the copper are increased to forty-eight. It must, however, be remembered that *thirty-six pounds of this is only water.* I would like to know who can conscientiously expect a horse to work well and continue in health on food which contains three hundred parts of water for every hundred of spoiled grain. It is an injustice to treat an animal in such a manner, which deserves more consideration on account of his usefulness, and whose better judgment would enable him to take water with greater comfort and benefit than can possibly accrue from deceiving him to swallow unlimited quantities in the form of a mess presenting such indescribable qualities and disproportionate quantities.

Cooked food for horses is a form which certainly has no analogy in nature, and wherever dictated, must inevitably arise from neglect or total ignorance of the anatomy of the digestive organs, with their physiology and the laws which govern assimilation.

To another objection raised against the cooked meat system, it is urged that horses so fed usually drink as much water as those confined to the dry meat or manger system. I believe there is truth in this as a rule, but the fact is not favourable to the plan, and great reasons may be assigned in the large quantities of common salt used in the mess, which occasions an unnatural thirst. Excess of common salt taken into the system proves highly injurious and predisposes the animal to disease, particularly of a congestive or low form, a condition of unnatural plethora being established.

The continued presence of sloppy food, besides acting—like bran mashes—as a foreign body, deranges the balance and harmony of vital functions generally, those of digestion primarily and particularly, and the large quantities of nutritious matter which may be present, having no admixture with natural secretions are not rendered assimilable. *It therefore proves an expensive mode of feeding.*

Nutritious matters not having undergone those necessary chemical and vital changes which are ensured by the secretions of the digestive organs, are not in a fit state to enter the blood. They may be taken up, but will act as a foreign body there as they do to the intestines, and must be expelled or communicate disease.

If they remain in the intestines, diarrhœa is induced by irritative action, and horses so fed void their dung much like a cow. Such a state in this animal is not proper order, and if allowed to go on, disease of some kind supervenes.

Errors to be Avoided.

On the other hand, if the unassimilated principle gains access to the blood, it is as soon as possible carried to the kidneys, and by them expelled. The animal frequently voids his urine. It will be frequently found to contain modified albumen, and even blood, and this accounts for the excessive number of cases of *diabetes* or *profuse staling* and *albuminuria* which have come under my notice during my residence in Glasgow.

Such cases are so common that they are considered trivial, and no doubt are, primarily; but when the errors of diet are allowed to proceed, they become marked by such characters as in the man wine-bibber and gourmand, or epicure, are modified, and appear as dyspepsia, biliousness, severe headache, piles, &c., a tolerable bloating of the countenance, with enlargement of the abdomen, which generally signifies organic disease.

The horse when suffering from these conditions is usually well drugged while at work, and as the same kind of feeding is persisted in, medicines repeatedly follow the aliment, the animal loses condition, and we may trace numerous instances of *farcy* and *glanders* to this as an undoubted cause.

Other terminations are dilated stomach, broken wind, congested, or schirrus liver, calculi (or stones) in the intestines, recurrent colic, organic disease of the kidneys and bladder, or probably speedy death from over-distention and fermentation of the contained food, causing rupture of the stomach, some part of the intestines, or diaphragm (midriff).

Advantages of proper Food and System.

My experience, and that of others who have devoted attention to the conditions discussed in the preceding section, clearly shows that the secret lies in *prevention*. This is comprised in cleanliness, ventilation, care and attention to the quality, quantity, and regularity of feeding, and due proportion of work.

The author is old enough to remember the effect of a journey from London to the north by stage coach, the character of animals selected for the work, and the amount they were required to perform. With such experiences he has frequently paused to enquire how the facts have failed to carry conviction in analogous cases at the present day.

In many of the coaches which ran between London, York, and Leeds, the horses were known to "do their fourteen miles out and the same number in" six days in the week. Their work was testified by the wear of the shoes, which, made of the toughest metal, and not unfrequently having an admixture of steel, were worn out by the fore feet in three weeks, and replaced on the hind by new ones nearly every fourteen days. Notwithstanding this, by proper feeding, care,

Advantages of proper Food and System. 47

and ventilation of the stables, these animals retained their health and usefulness for years. Among them was a celebrated mare, " Old Sal." She ran in one of the above coaches as " off wheeler " for years, was known by all upon the road, had never been sick a single day, and when railways revolutionized the system of transit was over twenty years of age, and even then " as fresh as paint."

When the fly-boats plied between Glasgow and Edinbro' on the Forth and Clyde Canal, an old mare named " Maggie Lauder," was stationed to run between Port Dundas and Glasgow Bridge, a distance of eight miles, the time allowed being one hour. After a rest of one hour the return journey to Port Dundas was made, and in the afternoon she performed the whole distance over again, thus travelling and drawing the boat thirty-two miles per day.

The person from whom I obtained my information rode the animal daily for seven years, during which time she was doing the work alluded to six days in the week, " was never sick nor sorry a single day, nor ever had a day's rest in addition to the usual Sunday."

When the boats were superseded by railways, "Maggie Lauder " was sold at the age of *twenty-nine years*.

A similar instance is related of a horse employed in like manner on the Paisley canal. He was sold at the age of twenty-seven when the boats were discontinued, and, being "fresh as a lark" at the time, suddenly fractured the bone of one of his legs in his gambols while being led home by his purchaser.

I am aware that breeding will in a measure account for "pluck" and disposition to work in animals as well as in man, but it will not stand in the place of *ability* under any circumstances. The willingness or pluck may be always present, but ability will depend upon a condition of strength.

One thorough-bred horse will resemble another very much in disposition, but differ widely in ability from mode of living. Take the first from the green pasture and run him alongside that brought direct from hard dry corn and sound hay, upon which he has subsisted months, and performed daily exertion. The effect is easily perceived; weight or distance is scarcely an object to him, but the first is blown or lamed before half a dozen fences are crossed, or has received his death summons from various causes.

Harness horses, and horses used in draught, require similar treatment to produce strength and endurance.

While pluck is derived from breeding, strength is derived from food and a healthy digestion. Corn and hay, transmuted within the penetralia of the living organism, becomes muscle. Manure, the refuse of digestion and the animal body, the

Advantages of proper Food and System. 49

agriculturist knows, nourishes his land, without which he can expect no crop. In the production of artificial light, all depends upon the supply of combustive material and agents which support or promote the process, which, in proportion to quantity and quality, afford a good or bad kind of illumination. In the warming of buildings the maximum temperature can only be obtained by instituting an operation of the laws of combustion upon materials capable of undergoing that process, and, likewise, by the operation of laws within the animal organism, if we need strength (force), it must first be supplied in the shape of sound, dry provender.

There is a very erroneous idea, at least to my perception, entertained by many, that where a draught horse is required for moving extreme weights he should be large and ponderous. If the dealer is enquired of, "You want weight," says he. If a friend be appealed to, a similar recommendation is given. It is in this way many useless, heavy-legged, unsightly, lugubrious, and slovenly animals are tolerated. What these are supposed to gain by superior capabilities in moving weights they lose in speed, and hence are seen creeping along the streets, and, as occurs in some towns, creating quite an obstruction to general traffic.

It appears to me that strength is required, not absolute weight, but a good development of

E

muscle. If weight only is wanted, it would not be so frequently remarked that horses "will not pull a sitting hen off her nest."

And, again, if nothing but weight will suffice, then a lump of lead or any inanimate object would answer equally as well.

I would refer my readers to Youatt's excellent treatise on draught, and they will perceive that other objections are against tall animals for moving loads, particularly on four-wheeled carriages.

Regular Feeding.

It is one of the essentials of good management that horses should receive their food as regularly as possible. Without regularity, and especially with long fasts, the digestive organs are prostrated or weakened, and food, which would otherwise be nutritious, brings about those changes already described.

In coal mines, where feeding and work is dictated by those who know nothing about it, broken wind, colic, diabetes, organic diseases of various kinds, calculi and death by rupture, are common. When, on the contrary, attention is given, these fatalities are rare, and when they occur are usually traced to other causes.*

---

* Much valuable information has from time to time been detailed to me by my friends, Mr. Charles Hunting, M.R.C.V.S., and Mr. Luke Scott, M.R.C.V.S., whose experience in the management of pit animals is of the most extensive character in Britain, and therefore to be received with respect.

Calculi or Stones in the Intestines.

The nature and aggregation of the particles which compose these bodies are not without interest, as affording information on the conditions which are present in the stomach and intestines. *Calculi* are very common in the horses and ponies of some coal mines, and also among the horses of millers, general carters, and those used in large establishments where the system of feeding and work is defective.

Their origin is usually considered to arise from water impregnated by the salts of lime, which are precipitated in the same manner from solution as occurs in the steam boiler or tea kettle.

It does not follow that calculi form on the use of such kind of water. It is also a most notorious fact that from water of precisely the same character supplied to the animals in two coal pits, different results are manifest. In one, where proper care in feeding and work is observed, there is the greatest amount of health, but in the other, where systems are the reverse, and especially when work is excessive and irregular, calculi exist.

That the water draining from the magnesian limestone, and holding lime in solution, has not much to do with their formation, is proved by several circumstances.

First: Many calculi which I have found in

such animals have little or no lime in their composition, being mainly composed of mucus, hair, dirt, coals, &c., closely matted together, and known as "*dust balls.*"

Second: The miners consume large quantities of the same water, but are not known to suffer from intestinal calculi.

Third: From personal experience and residence in districts where calcareous or hard waters only can be had, I have ascertained that calculi are not more prevalent when system is observed, and

Fourth: I have found calculi to exist more abundantly where water is of the purest character. Some of the largest specimens which have been obtained were from horses using soft water alone, and therefore must have another origin.

To attribute their formation to any special kind of water is a false theory, and negatives the power of the intestines to remove useless matter.

The presence of a nail, piece of wood, stone, or other hard substance, is also said to insure the formation of calculi. But horses and cattle meet with these things constantly among their food, and, while many are doubtless rejected by the sensitive lips, others are swallowed, as proved by their presence in the dung during life, or intestines after death.

The *origin* of the material which forms the substance of a stone or calculus is undoubtedly from the *food*. Hard waters may assist under certain circumstances.

Calculi or Stones in the Intestines. 53

They may contain a large quantity of lime, but the food relatively contains a much larger proportion. It is a substance largely in demand for the wants of the system.

If the animal is enfeebled by overtaxing work, long fasts, and supplied with food of an inferior quality, a condition known by the term *bulimia*, is established. This is known by an irregular, capricious, and morbid appetite, irregular bowels, staring coat, leanness, inaptitude for work, and a desire to lick the walls. Sometimes, however, these symptoms are either not well marked, or escape observation.

Under such circumstances the animal swallows sticks, stones, and rubbish of all kinds, to appease the ravenous desire within. Food, under these conditions, is not properly digested, the secretions are vitiated, or altogether deficient, and act imperfectly. Farther derangement occurs, in which the liver particularly suffers, and affairs now assume an aggravated character.

During these conditions assimilation and absorption is not carried on perfectly, and the mineral matters of food and water are deposited in the solid form, and aggregate around any rough surface or object which may be present.

As the mass increases in size corresponding derangement is continued, and thus secures material for its development, or the formation of others—as many as fifty having been found in one animal.

Some time may elapse before acute symptoms are observed. Suddenly abdominal pain arises. Symptoms are continued, and become aggravated, admitting of no relief, and the animal dies.

Upon making a *post-mortem* examination, one or more of these stones are found to have passed into a narrow part of the gut, and become imprisoned by spasmodic action of the muscular walls which tightly enclose it on all sides. Sometimes destruction of the gut has occurred, and the stone is partially or wholly liberated along with the contents of the intestines.*

Objections to the Use of Dry Food.

It is urged by many persons enthusiastic in the feeding and management of horses, that a change

---

* I have succeeded in obtaining a great number of these interesting specimens during the past sixteen years. In less than two years twenty-six were obtained from pit animals, having caused death, and many more were found in animals dying from other causes.

Their composition was principally mucus, the felted down from the oat, silicious matter and carbonate of lime. The last-named substance usually formed the outer portion, while the interior was filled by pieces of coal mixed with the other ingredients. Many of these were presented to the museum of the Albert Veterinary College, London.

Several fine specimens have recently been forwarded to me by my friend, Mr. Thomas Foreman, M.R.C.V.S., Leadgate, Durham, exhibiting similar peculiarities. Of these he has collected a great number from pit animals.

Objections to the Use of Dry Food. 55

to a system of bruising and cutting of food gains only one advantage, *viz.*, the animal fills his stomach quicker, and is thereby enabled to take more rest.

This property is pre-eminently claimed in favour of cooked food, and in addition, that it is partially digested for the animal. Experience and systematic enquiry prove the fallacy of these tenets.

I have shown that digestion, when properly carried on, is wonderfully rapid and effective.

The stomach, being small, is rapidly emptied again. This obtains in all horses, including those fed on the *manger system*.

Every one knows the effects of bran mashes. How much more, then, must constant supplies of food, supposed to be half digested at commencement, containing much water, and being an unnatural mixture, act like a foreign body?

The laws of the animal economy render such results inevitable, for as quickly, in proportion, as the stomach is voiding the digestible portions, the sensation of hunger arises, and desire for food is appeased by taking in more. Thus it will be found, in opposition to the argument in favour of a half-digested food, that the process of digestion is accelerated, and more is required. Such food always fails to give up the whole of its nutrition; *the animal eats more, costs also more, and gains the least by the method.*

It is thus that an equally long time is occupied

Objections to the Use of Dry Food.

in the consumption of food, and visit him at any hour of the night, he will be found having an appetite, and like Oliver Twist, "looking for more."

Rapidity of digestion is a provision established by nature. If the stomach had been from the first intended to receive the large quantities frequently placed before horses, or to perform functions assigned to the teeth and salivary glands in addition to its own, the logical inference is that, as nature, in her development of all things, has not studied ornament merely, the stomach would have been endowed with greater capacity and powers, and teeth and salivary glands in all probability absent entirely.

It is also urged against the dry meat or manger system, that horses fail to masticate or grind the whole of their corn, that much in a state capable of germination or growth passes out in the excrement, and, of course, the cooked meat system supplies this deficiency.

During a season of extreme scarcity in India, it has been stated,* the famine-hunted wretches followed the English camp, and drew their principal nourishment from the grains of corn extracted from the excrement of horses.

I well remember an extensive firm employing many horses, whose manure was objected to by

---

* Letter from an Indian officer to J. Curwen, M.P., quoted in Blaine's (fifth) edition of "The Veterinary Art."

Objections to the Use of Dry Food. 57

several farmers because they obtained crops of oats in places where they were not required, after using it on the land. I have also observed the heap of manure literally covered with green blades from the growing oats. How was this, and why has such a simple circumstance had no better effect than to induce a system of porridge feeding for an animal eminently unfitted for it?

It was in this wise. The remedy was sought for in a manner too superficially; and in the absence of an acquaintance with the principles of management, the horse has been compelled to suffer for the omissions of others.

In such cases I have known carpenters, and even more unlikely men appealed to for information and a remedy. The system resembles very much that so commonly adopted under certain Acts of Parliament, where discretion and power is given to tailors, joiners, bailiffs, policemen *et hoc genus omne*, to pronounce in a magisterial court what is cruelty to animals in a medical point of view, and to descant upon the pathological signs which prove a carcass to be diseased, and all this in the teeth of an educated scientific witness.

Such matters require dealing with philosophically. They are not within the comprehension of every clodhopper, groom, and coachman, who fancies he knows all about a horse because he cleans him. Their duties lie in the practical administration of the brush and broom, and faithful

58 Objections to the Use of Dry Food.

execution of all orders entrusted to them. Management and dictation form no part of these.

The internal arrangements of the horse and all domestic animals require the assistance of brains not so illiterate, and if they were properly supplied with such, the horse and his master would enjoy a much longer acquaintance.

It is important to us to enquire whether oats or any kind of grain are capable of growing after having passed through from eighty to ninety feet of intestines subjected to healthy acid, alkaline, and other peculiar juices which convert their starch into sugar, separate and modify their albumen and caseine, and dissolve out salts, or to a temperature varying from $98°$ to $102°$ F., occupying time varying from ten to twenty-four hours?

I venture to predict not, and to assert that very few grains will pass out unacted upon. If such were the case the whole processes of mastication, insalivation, digestion, and that of making malt are but a farce, and cannot be accounted for by the present deductions of science.

The solution of the growing oats, however, was soon made apparent.

The manger system had been imperfectly carried on for some time without any alteration in the size or character of the mangers themselves. These were shallow, narrow, and not provided with cross-bars. In this way much was

Objections to the Use of Dry Food. 59

wasted by the horses throwing out the corn when searching for better portions.

In addition, I entered the stables on one occasion when the premises were supposed to be deserted, and observed a number of those young urchins who are always a kind of *sine qua non* about lorries and stables, carrying on a mimic warfare, the missiles in the case being oats, obtained from the open corn-bin or granary. It was afterwards ascertained this had been a common practice. The successful remedy soon followed in the shape of deep and wide mangers, with iron cross-bars, padlocks to the corn-bin and granary door, and institution of a proper room for mixing the corn and cut food.

That the half-famished Indians picked something out of the excrements of the horses I have no doubt, and they most probably resembled oats in appearance. Birds, especially sparrows and common fowls, are also captivated to make such a selection for their crop. But only in outward appearance would these abstracted matters resemble the grain of oats. Few have trusted themselves and their judgment in troubling in this matter farther than making the broad assertion on the strength of appearances. A superficial mode, and very delusive proposition to be circulated. I have tested the matter and found it to be an error.

If the stomach and digestive organs generally are in a state of health and order, very few grains escape their action, and the common inference is that if the horses of the Indian campaign referred to really parted with so much corn as to support such a number of followers, they must have been fed in a very imperfect manner, their digestive organs in a state of disorder, and from the loss of the food, in a condition certainly not desirable in an enemy's country.

In France the subject met with the attention of Boussingault and Papin, who instituted experiments, and ascertained correctly that the passage of undigested grain from the bowels of horses in health is merely nominal.

Out of eight pounds allowed per diem only one ounce of unchanged grain could be detected, and this weight included moisture.

The digestive organs generally should be in a state of healthy action in order to secure the proper benefit from food.

Under this head there requires little to be written. I have fully shown how disease originates by false management, and how waste occurs in food supplied under such circumstances. It must, therefore, be apparent that those organs specially set apart for providing the fabric of the animal body should not be overtaxed or enfeebled. If such occurs the whole body suffers more or less.

Care is especially needed after protracted hard work and long fasts, avoiding the use of large

Objections to the Use of Dry Food. 61

quantities of cold water upon the contents of a well-filled stomach, or supplying too much food at one time. In fact these precautions would repay, if followed, at all times; neglect of them is a frequent source of derangement, and from which fatal consequences usually succeed.

Where a great number of horses are kept it is far more profitable to employ a person whose sole occupation is confined to the feeding department. Corn, &c., should be transferred to his possession under proper rules for mixture and use, the quantities being accurately stated in documents handed to him. In return he should furnish evidence of having carefully complied with the terms, and his papers should also afford particular information as to consumption under all circumstances, regular or variable.

He should be a man who will carefully notice the condition of all horses when brought to the stable, and willing to minister to their comfort in properly regulating the quantity of food each may receive without injury.

The details of such management require special attention in order to be properly applied to the various circumstances which obtain in different establishments. There is, however, no particular difficulty beyond a willingness that need be encountered, in order to make the whole safe, satisfactory, and profitable.

In the absence of particulars it would be an

Objections to the Use of Dry Food.

impossibility to attempt to lay down a plan suitable for any particular establishment. An outline must be framed on the principles here given, the work, size, and nature of animal, &c., being points of importance for consideration.

PART II.

Varieties of Food.

The food used for working horses are those cereals and leguminous seeds which, usually denominated corn, consist of oats, barley, Indian corn or maize, peas, beans, and tares, together with hay, straw, bran, and linseed.

These vary much in their properties as well as nutrition, and on that ground alone arises the question " What kinds are best, and what proportion should be given ?"

An answer will greatly depend upon circumstances, such as the character of work imposed, together with the market price and condition of the provender.

The relative proportions of nutritious matter contained in different kinds of food have been ascertained from time to time by analysis, an outline of which is as follows :—

In 100 pounds.	Nutritious matter.	Fat, or heat producers.
Turnips	1	9
Red beet	$1\frac{1}{2}$	$8\frac{1}{2}$
Carrots	2	10
Potatoes	2	25
Hay	8	$68\frac{1}{2}$

Varieties of Food.

In 100 pounds.	Nutritious matter.	Fat, or heat producers.
Maize, or Indian corn	12	67
Oats	14	68
Barley	18	$68\frac{1}{2}$
Bran	18	4
Linseed	24	$64\frac{3}{4}$
Beans	31	$51\frac{1}{2}$
Peas	32	$51\frac{1}{2}$
Tares, or lentils	33	48

Maize or Indian Corn.—By the above table it will be observed that maize among corn contains the least percentage of nutritious matter, and from it we gather that it is not suited as a principal article of diet for working animals. It contains a great proportion of water and starchy matters, and forms in consequence an excellent food for pigs and fatting animals, given with other varieties.

Oats stand next in proportion, and by custom have been most commonly selected as a principal article of diet for horses, but prove very expensive as sometimes used. This is very apparent on calculation, and results are demonstrative in practice.

A horse doing little work, or what actually only amounts to exercise, would be economically and advantageously fed upon hay and oats, as the demand for muscular power not being great, such articles form a very suitable diet, without causing him to become overloaded with fat and a burden to himself.

Varieties of Food.

Estimating oats to weigh 42lbs. per bushel, and costing twenty-six shillings per quarter (eight bushels), the cost per week for different allowances, together with the amount of nutritious matter contained, would be somewhat as follows:—

Pounds per day.	Pounds per week.	Cost. s. d.	Azotised or nutritious matter in pounds.
10	70	5 5	9·8
12	84	6 6	11·76
14	98	7 7	13·52
16	112	8 8	15·68
18	126	9 9	17·64
20	140	10 10	19·60

In addition, sixpence must be added for each stone (14lbs.) of hay consumed, which yields 11·20 oz. of nutritious matter.

Oats should be heavy in the hand, devoid of thick husks, and short and plump in the kernel. Good dry potato or Scotch oats, weighing 39 to 42 pounds per bushel, are undoubtedly cheapest to purchase at all times, and to be preferred to other kinds weighing from 33 to 37 pounds, even when four or five shillings extra per quarter is paid.

It is no saving to purchase corn, especially oats, *made up* to a certain weight. Some dealers guarantee four bushels of oats for a stated price to weigh, say 160 pounds, and when measured

F

the quantity considerably exceeds the four bushels.

Under such circumstances the purchase cannot be as beneficial as if the oats were 160 lbs. natural weight. The inference is, the grain is of an inferior quality, the kernel being light and the husks disproportionately heavy. *It is always more profitable to obtain standard measure and weight,* as this proves an important item in twelve months, and particularly when animals are doing variable work.

The lower priced oats may answer well for moderate exercise or work, but as soon as the labour is increased, or a change is made from standard weighing oats to others of a lower nutritious per centage, animals suddenly fall away in condition, and become liable to disease, and in ignorance of the real causes, are not unfrequently impregnated with a course of useless and even dangerous drugs. It is thus the expenses of feeding are obviously increased, as to them are to be added less ability for work, and an additional incurring of expense, while the original cost of the provender is really but a fraction below the price of good material.

When the kernel of oats is small the husk preponderates, the former containing as low as eight per cent. only of nutritious matter, and the latter no better than straw itself, but for which the price of oats is paid.

Mr. Hunting proved this by a set of tedious

Varieties of Food. 67

but ingenious experiments. He says * "One ounce of foreign oats, 39lbs. per bushel, was weighed, the same weight of old Scotch, 40lbs. per bushel, and the same weight of Tartar oats 36lbs. per bushel. The foreign oats contained 1,112 kernels, the Scotch oats, 1,084, and the Tartars, 1,144. The husks were weighed. The husks of the 1,144 grains of Tartars weighed 120 grains; of the 1,112 kernels of foreign oats, 126 grains; while the husk of the 1,084 kernels of Scotch only weighed 96 grains."

Under these circumstances, horses fed upon three bushels of oats per week, weighing 42lbs. per bushel, would receive 126lbs. total weight, of which 25lbs. would be husks, having a value only of four per cent., in nutritious matter.

Change this to Tartar oats at 39lbs. per bushel, exactly 39lbs. must be extracted for husks, and if the foreign oats are used, 36lbs. would be the amount of husk in the same quantity.

It must be borne in mind that the inferior kinds of oats are not only remarkable for a preponderance of husk, but their nutritious matter, and consequently their feeding qualities, are considerably below the standard weighing Scotch oats.

Similar rules should be applied to other kinds of grain or corn, and their standard qualities

---

* "On the Feeding and Management of our Domestic Animals." p. 14.

obtained from analyses upon which reliance can be placed, and information will thus be easily obtained whereby to institute a system of mixtures for any purpose of feeding.

Selection and Purchase of Grain.

Most persons are aware that corn should be thoroughly dry for feeding purposes, otherwise inconveniences occur in the form of indigestion, colic, weed, grease, or loss of condition, &c.

Besides, in purchasing that which is not dry, or seasoned, a decided loss occurs, which buyers should avoid by securing a reduced price in accordance.

Owing to this, large feeders take advantage of the markets, and purchase oats, peas, beans, barley, &c., as they are aware that in good corn the loss by a reasonable evaporation of water is an ample payment for the construction of granaries for spreading out and constantly turning; added to which, animals are kept in better condition, and work is less interfered with by illness on that account.

I have known hundreds of quarters of corn purchased under such conditions, and with the observance of other measures, to be noticed, a balance has been shown which has cleared the cost of keeping the animals for a great portion of the time, as compared with the previous cost from another mode of feeding.

Selection and Purchase of Grain.

The purchase of grain should not be referred to week, month, or year, in fact, to no period if it can be avoided. It is much better to store up corn and ensure it being thoroughly dry, than to depend upon purchase when it is immediately required. Many good bargains are put in the way of owners who are open to purchase, and the profit obtained helps to improve the appearance of the credit side of the balance sheet.

Where roomy grain floors cannot be had, it becomes a matter of greater necessity that the provender should be dry, and of *guaranteed weight and measure*. Of a necessity also, a higher price must be paid for it, and even under those circumstances it answers far better than the use of inferior kinds. To constant purchasers, dealers are to be found who will endeavour to provide what is required in the shape of a regular sample, and thus difficulties are greatly overcome.

These principles have been more understood of late by those who feed large numbers of horses, and whose competitive kind of work requires them to study every item of expenditure. In some instances animals are fed inexpensively, and preserve their health and condition with remarkable benefit from the system, even under much harder work.

Economy of Food.

The method of economising food consists in using *a variety of grain* instead of one kind, and that exclusively oats. Some have tried the different leguminous kinds also separately, but found them inefficient in economy, and even injurious.

A farmer of my acquaintance having about thirty horses, purchased, at a cheap rate, a quantity of Indian corn, under the idea that it would effect a saving in the cost of feeding. On the contrary, the health and condition were greatly sacrificed.

Others, again, give a preponderance of beans, acting upon the well known fact that, being more nutritive than oats, they must be more economical. In the mode adopted, however, they have proved highly expensive as well as injurious.

Linseed is also added, and with pernicious results. It is too laxative for general use in quantity, but judiciously administered proves assimilative, hastens the process of assimilation, and assists in the formation of fat and flesh. As a nutritious body it is very highly expensive.

Tares, which are the most nutritious diet we can use for horses, are objectionable as being unpalatable in quantity. Similar objections may be urged against other varieties of food when exclusively used, particularly in their liability to produce disorder of the digestive organs.

Economy of Food. 71

A mixture, therefore, should be regulated by special conditions. Due consideration is to be given to the nutritious matter contained in each ingredient, and as a whole, the amount and character of the work, quantity allowed to each animal, and the price paid at the time. Where the consumer is compelled to go to the dealer for his week's, fortnight's, or month's supply, this is particularly needed, as there is no room for speculation on the rise or fall of corn, upon which frequently large sums are to be saved.

In estimating the amount of nutritious matter contained in food of different kinds, and how much is required to preserve horses in health under their work, the table given in pages 63, 64 will be found of great service. Practically, it is answered by observing the quantity of oats of standard nutrition, or other kind of food, which may be required to keep the animals in condition for work and perfect health. The amount of nutritious matter is then determined according to the per centage stated opposite each kind by simple rule of three. This done, the estimate of nutrition contained in other kinds is observed, and mixtures arranged, forms of which will shortly be submitted.

It is to be next inquired, will this ensure a less cost than is incurred by the principal use of oats? The answer is emphatically, yes, and with a greater supply of nutrition.

I am indebted to a gentleman of great experience among horses for valuable information in the feeding of his animals.

They are employed in the town of Sheffield, which is not unlike Glasgow for its hills.

The work is severe, and consists in removing the heavy manufactures of steel, stoves, hardware, &c., to and from the railway station. Drays or lorries are generally used, and three tons is a common load.

In a letter to me dated April 4th, 1864, he says:—

"Our horses' diet is as follows:—

Hay	16 pounds per day,	8 stones per week.
Oats	10 ,, ,,	5 ,, ,,
Beans ...	5 ,, ,,	$2\frac{1}{2}$,, ,,
Maize ...	4 ,, ,,	2 ,, ,,
Bran	2 ,, ,,	1 ,, ,,
Total .	37 ,, ,,	$18\frac{1}{2}$,, ,,

No loose hay, all is chopped; oats, beans, Indian corn all crushed separately, then the whole is mixed with the chop. The hay costs 4s. per cwt., oats, 1s. per stone,* maize, 11d., beans, 1s. 2d., and bran $7\frac{1}{2}d.$ per stone.

"I always buy of the best quality without regard to price, as I find that the cheapest, all points considered. As a rule, I greatly prefer English oats.† The harvest of 1862 was an

---

* The hundredweight is 112 lbs., the stone 14 lbs.

† I think the term English is here applied without prejudice

Economy of Food. 73

exception, and I bought foreign oats principally, being in a superior condition to English. In addition to the above—which is the winter scale, the summer is somewhat reduced—we every Saturday night give each horse a mash of linseed mixed with a small proportion of bran, boiled altogether and given warm.

" This serves to lubricate and clear the bowels, and comforts the animals. I do not know whether that is the cause; but since its adoption we have had few, if any, cases of colic, or severe inflammation; prior to the adoption of that system these cases were of great occurrence."

It must be borne in mind that these are heavy horses, and we have here also an evidence from an unprejudiced source, that a considerable amount of nutritious matter is required to keep up the health and condition of the animals, since when the inferior kinds of mixture were supplied, in the shape of oats principally, disease was common. This I can testify, having been in professional attendance.

We are also taught practically that a loss of condition and proneness to disease is brought about by food containing too little nutrition, when the demands upon the system are excessive.

---

to Scotch oats, but as a distinction to foreign and inferior kinds. The writer is keenly alive to the qualities of the various kinds of corn, having had unlimited experience in the feeding and management of the best draught horses in large numbers, and doing the hardest work.

74 Systems adopted on various Colliery Estates.

Suppose these animals had been fed exclusively upon oats and hay, they would require to consume weekly *four-and-a-half bushels* of the former, and about *ten stones* of the latter, in order to receive the same amount of nutrition, viz. $31\frac{1}{2}$ pounds derived from the mixture quoted, and which would cost at the same prices about *eighteen shillings and sixpence*.

Here is also a decided saving of three shillings and sixpence per horse per week, by the use of the mixture, which only costs *fifteen shillings*, and with fifty horses would realize £8 15s., and for a year £455, besides almost an immunity from disease and death, to which they were before exposed.

Systems adopted on various Colliery Estates.

It is by paying particular attention to these matters that so much has been effected in the saving over former expenditure, on many colliery establishments, where the supply and mixing of grain is under the management of the veterinary surgeon.

Mr. Hunting, in his pamphlet already referred to, has shown that with the number of horses and ponies employed at the various collieries of the South Hetton Coal Company—all doing the hardest work—the saving effected in ten years amounted to no less than the enormous sum of

Cut Food in Promoting Insalivation. 75

£31,876 2s. 7½d. by cutting the hay into chaff and mixing with small quantities of straw, and substituting superior kinds of beans, peas, barley, tares, &c., in lieu of oats. He also states that out of 225 horses employed in two pits, during six weeks between 15th December, 1850, and 24th January, 1851, when the old system was pursued, there died of colic and its consequences *three horses and ponies;* while with the same number of animals under the improved *régime* during seven years, there were *less than three cases per annum.*

Cut Food as an Agent in Promoting proper Insalivation.

The value of this kind of provender as an agent in causing a proper insalivation of food is undoubted. On this subject Mr. Hunting is as explicit as he is full of information regarding it. He found that a number of animals, all selected as near as possible with an average age, height, and common appetite, required much longer time to consume the same weight and measure of food cut and mixed in the manger than when it was given in the shape of long hay in the rack, and oats only in the manger, from ten to thirteen minutes more being required.

After what has been said in reference to the objects of the teeth and salivary glands and their

Cut Food in Promoting Insalivation.

secretions, it must be obvious that in giving food in its naturally dry state, it serves more important uses in the animal economy. And as the *quantity* of saliva plays also an equally important part, the use of cut food is here unmistakably shown to be a very desirable proceeding.

At the *Hetton Colliery*, Mr. Luke Scott, M.R.C.V.S. has followed out most useful principles. His attention had been arrested in 1851 by the inefficiency of the existing system of feeding, and proneness to mortality which was constant among the horses and ponies employed.

The quantities allowed per pay* to each animal employed in connection with the estate were as follows :—

	Oats in Bushels.	Cost. £ s. d.	Hay in stones.	Cost. s.	Total. £ s. d.
Waggon Horse .	8	1 6 0	28	14	2 0 0
Farm Horse .	6	19 6	20	10	1 9 6
Pit Horse .	6	19 6	24	12	1 11 6
Pit Pony .	3	9 9	12	6	15 9

It is necessary to state, the whole of the hay here allowed was not consumed. Much is constantly wasted in collieries by being carelessly sent down the pits, or conveyed to the stables in large trusses, which come in contact with water, dirt, and grease. The animals consequently refuse it, and generally place it beneath them, sufficient being

---

* Colliery accounts in the county of Durham are made up once a fortnight, when wages are paid; hence the term " pay."

frequently gathered to make a very good bed. I have seen a week's supply of hay and corn lying exposed to the dust flying from the pit mouth, as well as steam, condensing as it falls from the boilers, and, in common instances, to the rain of one or two nights in addition, before being sent down. The former kind of unsystematic arrangement was of frequent occurrence at one pit, but no kind of remonstrance succeeded in effecting an alteration.

Pit animals are usually kept *twelve hours* at work, and in many cases, *without food and water*,* or at least without a satisfactory amount of either, and seldom periods of rest.

I have known animals kept from their stable thirty-six hours at a time, and when complaints have been made they have been met with a stout denial from the powers that be; or, where denial has been useless, it has been assigned as a cause, that the veterinary surgeon has not provided a sufficient number of animals for the working of the pit, an office which he does not include among his duties without express orders.†

Such long fasts act very prejudicially upon

---

* The practice is not so common as formerly. In some pits it is abolished, but slumbers in others.

† Lord Kinnaird, in his letter to the Home Secretary on the Fearndale Colliery explosion, dated 15th November, 1867, has fully shown the aspect of colliery affairs when he quotes the words of the miner, who says, "If peoples as knows dared to speak, these things would soon be stopped."

the animal. When he returns to the stable the food is seized and ravenously swallowed, and, as a consequence, it does the least good, but is more frequently productive of the greatest harm.

By a reference to previous remarks on the estimate of nutritious matter in the various articles of food, it will be found that the Hetton Colliery "old plan" of feeding was doubly expensive and extravagant. It was innutritious as it yielded to the wagon horse (and others proportionately) one fourth less nutriment than the mixture given hereafter. It was expensive because it cost nineteen shillings per week, from its use much was wasted, the animals were in bad condition, and mortality great.

It was decided at length, to allow Mr. Scott to regulate the system, which he did, in the following way :—

His first act was to have the hay cut in trusses of sufficient size to fit a coal tub,* in which they are sent down the pit, and thus totally prevented from collecting dirt and grease as before. This resulted in a saving of the amount wasted, and also supply in a better condition, which would be turned to account in the animal body.

The varieties of grain fixed upon to be used were bruised separately, and mixed in the following proportions :—

---

* This plan is also carried out at all the collieries under Mr. Hunting's superintendence.

Cut Food in Promoting Insalivation. 79

Grain.	Weight per bush. lbs.	Price per qr. s.	Actual weight. lbs.	Cost. s.
Barley, 4 bushels	56	30	224	15
Oats, 4 ,,	42	26	168	13
Peas, 2 ,,	66	40	132	10
			524	£1 18

In order to arrive at an average number of animals to be fed, the ponies and horses in the pits are classed as follows:—

All above 15 hands are called horses.

Three above 13 hands, and under 15 hands, equal to two horses.

Two above 11 hands, and under 13 hands, equal to one horse.

Under this arrangement the whole were reduced to an average of 130 horses.

The superiority of the system is at once apparent by a reference to the subjoined analysis, in which the two plans are contrasted.

Old System, for One Pit Horse.

6 bushels of oats per pay, at 3s. 3d.	19s. 6d.
24 stones of hay, at 6d.	12s. 0d.
	£1 11s. 6d.
Or for 26 pays (one year)	£40 19s. 0d.
Nutritious matter contained	52·08 lbs.

Cut Food in Promoting Insalivation.

New System, for One Pit Horse.

176 lbs. of the mixture	14s. 4d.
18 stones of hay, at 6d.	9s. 0d.
21 pounds of bran	11d.
Total per pay	£1 4s. 3d.
Or for 26 pays (one year)	£31 10s. 6d.
Saving effected for one horse for one year	9 8s. 6d.
Cost per horse under old plan	£40 19s. 0d.
Saving in 130 horses for one year	£1225 5s. 0d.
Nutritious matter contained	48·18 lbs.

In the old system it will be observed that 52·08 lbs. of N.M. (nutritious matter) are contained in the food supplied, against 48·18 lbs. in the new. The greater part, however, was not obtained by the animals on account of the excessive waste already mentioned in the hay, and from the greedy manner in which the corn was devoured.

The additional 4 lbs. of N.M. supplied also proved expensive, besides useless, as it was unavailable. For it the sum of 7s. 3d. per pay was being paid, as forming part of a system which engendered disease, and gave the animals even less support, although professedly, a mode which furnished a large amount.

It is now a custom to allow the pit animals a portion of the hay and corn during the day, instead of causing them to fast twelve hours, as before.

The result is, Mr. Scott has found that the food is more leisurely taken, masticated, and thoroughly digested.

Besides the saving effected in actual expenditure, the reduction of disease and losses by death, is an important item. In repeated visits to the animals in the pits fed upon Mr. Scott's principle, it is due from me to state that I never saw a greater uniformity in condition while the hardest work was being imposed, and cases of indigestion, colic, and death in consequence, were the exception, and of extremely rare occurrence.

What constitutes a Cheap Food.

It is usually considered a cheap mode of feeding, when material can be supplied for one penny per pound, and I find several owners base their calculations of cost at this rate. But it must be borne in mind that food costing only one penny per pound is not inevitably an economical food. We must look farther than mere cost. Economy does not consist in price alone, to such must be added the veterinary surgeon's account, whose services in the main will be found to have been occasioned by the supposed economical food, and in addition, the value of the amount wasted by refusal, fermentation, or that which is hastened through the bowels in the state of "partial digestion," so much insisted upon.

Again, the amount of nutritious matter contained must be accurately calculated, or no reliable estimate of cheapness can be made. I am aware of several large firms in Glasgow who believe they are feeding economically upon one penny per pound rates, while their food yields ten per cent. less nutrition than the preceding mixtures, and cases of acute indigestion, &c., &c., are constant and numerous. These form a good comparison with the systems of Messrs. Hunting and Scott, the mixture proposed by the latter costing only ninety-eight parts of a penny per pound, with a high scale of nutritive value.

Objections to a change of Grain.

It is frequently urged that to adopt a total change in the kind of grain used, is to produce serious evils and fatal disorder, as exemplified by animals gaining access to the open corn bin, or to a heap of wheat or barley, when either rupture of the diaphragm, stomach, or intestines takes place, and death speedily ensues, while at other times founders (laminitis) occurs.

These certainly appear grave objections at first sight, but in reality are difficulties of no moment. We are speaking of *systematic* feeding, *not* deliberate engorgement. Death or disease results in one case by repletion and fermentation consequent upon the bolting of an unnatural quantity of food, which, if taken under proper principles, would in the other prove nutritious and life supporting. The death of horses by these means is fully carried out in analogy among mankind, with the exception that in the latter gluttony generally exerts itself a little more slowly.

In no case, with proper caution, will evil consequences ensue by a change to the dry, or manger system, from any other. It need therefore cause no apprehension.

Nature, Uses, and Abuses of Bran.

Bran will be found by analysis to contain from 14 to 18 per cent. of azotised matter, equal in fact to oats or barley. In nutrition, however, it is inferior to the straw of wheat or barley, a property which appears to obtain with the husk of grain generally. Owing to some peculiar form of combination, the azotised matter is not liberated by the process of digestion; hence those who consume bread in which the bran of wheat has been retained, under the idea that such is more nutritious, are greatly mistaken. The fæces or excrement are loaded with bran which has passed out almost unchanged, and horses fed upon it exhibit the same conditions.

That an admixture of bran with wheaten flour

or with the provender of horses, is useful and even profitable, there can be no doubt. This is to be attributed to the mechanical action set up by the siliceous particles, which obviates constipation, and preserves the proper action of the digestive organs when given in a judicious manner. Messrs. Hunting and Scott take advantage of this property, and use it *daily* with their superior mixtures of corn.

As *a laxative*, bran is justly called into requisition periodically as a warm mash for animals in whom there exists an innate disposition to constipation. I place the action of a bran mash, *given occasionally*, as one of the safest, most natural, and acceptable adjuncts towards the preservation of health; which effect is produced with more benefit and less deterioration to the system than by any other means. There are few horses that will not take it when offered as a change, and I would recommend, especially in winter, that it be given at the temperature of new milk, *not cold*, and the use of it should not be insisted upon indiscriminately, or ill effects are speedily shown.

Nothing can be more anomalous than the opinion entertained on the use of bran, as it obtains in many quarters. Believed to be non-nutritious, it is given largely during disease, to ward off critical inflammation, which a diet of corn might increase, but why it is persisted in with animals suffering from general prostration and weakening complaints is quite paradoxical.

It too often occurs also, when no appetite exists, it is paraded continually before the creature, and lies in the manger fouling the wood-work by fermentation, which the animal shows his repugnance to by standing as far back as his chain will allow.

System pursued at the Londonderry Collieries.

The horses and ponies employed at the collieries of the late Marchioness of Londonderry (now Earl Vane's), during my appointment as Veterinary Surgeon to her Ladyship, and subsequently for a short period to the Earl, were fed upon oats and peas—five parts of the former to one of the latter. The mixture was, however, never regulated by weighing. It was quite of an extemporary character, and entire guess work, a dash of peas being hastily put into the bottom of a "*poke*," and afterwards covered to the top with bruised oats, and the *whole* then weighed. In addition, hay, and green food in summer, was allowed, the cost of which I find by returns in my possession, amounted to £1 3s. 10½d. per horse per pay, all ponies being classed as two equal to one horse.

Under this arrangement 106 horses and 322 ponies exclusively employed in producing coal, and of course below ground principally, would in round numbers give 267 horses, the cost of feeding each being £31 0s. 9d. per annum.

At first sight this appears, and is really believed to be a very economical rate of feeding, being lower than Mr. Scott's expenditure at Hetton-lehole. Quality, however, is the test of cheapness, not the price alone at which the food is supplied. This allowance yields not more than 37·52 pounds of nutritious matter—assuming the one part of peas are carefully added, which I have grave reasons to doubt—against 48·18 in Mr. Scott's feed, in which 10·66 lbs. extra are supplied each pay per horse during the year, for which he incurs a cost only of 9s. 9d., the difference per horse per year.

But, as in the case of the old system at Hettonle-hole, the animals do not derive the whole of even this limited amount of benefit from the corn allowed. In winter *steamed food*, consisting of hay, linseed, and the one-fifth part of peas abstracted from the mixture, are supplied. This is sent down the pits during the afternoon, and frequently before the animals reach the stable in which the mess has been deposited by the horse-keeper, I have found it undergoing fermentation. Some, in fact many, of the animals refused it even when fresh, and from these causes the most nutritious portions were lost to them.

The process of steaming was conducted at separate places contiguous to a number of collieries, and the food conveyed in boxes or coaltubs placed in carts, and throughout the distance a dark-coloured fluid drained in profusion, of course carrying with it some of the most useful soluble principles of the food.*

The process of steaming food may answer well where inferior food and hay abound, cattle are to be fed, and aged dependants require some light employment. But as applied to good food, and carried out in the manner alluded to, it is a complete farce, a useless addition to expenditure —which, by the bye, is not made to appear in connection with the feeding—and deprivation to the hard-working animals. In fact, the whole system of feeding is no better, hence the number of cases of colic and indigestion, rapid falling away in condition, diabetes, &c., &c., which occur, and not being required to be reported at headquarters nothing is known of them. But if the gentlemen who attempt to feed horses without visiting them at their work or in their stables, and others who rule with pens and ink in a comfortable office, had to ride off at all hours in all kinds of weather three, six,.eight, or ten miles, descend a coal-mine, remain in the heated atmosphere several hours, and take the place of their coachman *outside* the conveyance in the cold night air, after influences equal to a severe

---

* In a visit to a large estate owned by a noble earl, where feeding is supposed to be conducted upon scientific principles, steamed food forms a large item for cattle. After the process is carried sufficiently far the food is removed, and the fluid accumulated from the condensed steam, containing useful soluble matters, is allowed to drain away in the gutter, while the animals are supplied with water for drinking. *Cui bono?*

vapour bath, each would perceive the advisability of reform. As such irregularities are in a coalpit hundreds of feet below the surface, they *do not see*, and it is very useful to be *determined not to see*.

With the exercise of common knowledge a man may be expert at purchasing corn, and make good bargains, but it requires a little more than that to adapt a proper system to the constantly varying wants of a large number of animals. If the principles of dieting and management require no more philosophy, and can be conducted with success without presence or information, the sooner such gentlemen take up also the treatment of disease by a system of telegraphy the better, and probably they may then make both ends meet still more satisfactorily to themselves.

From a strict examination of all phases and conditions, as they exist on that estate in common with many others, a more highly nutritious diet can be guaranteed—a reduction of disease and mortality therefrom to a minimum by the exercise of care and watchfulness, and these with a saving of *hundreds of pounds annually*.

The principle is of easy calculation. In large numbers, say three or four hundred animals, if two or three shillings only per week can be saved, it is a large sum at the end of the year. With other agencies it may also be increased. But on collieries there are objections to figures, except when they are used by the powers that be, and reports, although desired, are as waste paper. Like the phœnix, however, these may rise from their ashes, and, under another name, with an official envelope, appear as new and *original* creatures altogether.

In leaving this part of the subject, I would enquire how it is possible for a pit horse of fifteen or sixteen hands, with his large muscular system—doing from twenty to thirty miles a day, drawing a train of coal tubs, one way empty the other laden with many tons, in a highly heated and dusty atmosphere, and perspiring freely—to obtain sufficient nutriment from an allowance of twelve pounds of oats per day. The same is allowed to many carriage horses, and those of our cavalry regiments receive it within a fraction, for which exertion amounting to healthy and necessary exercise only, compared with the work of a pit horse, is exacted.

Other Forms of Admixture.

I have shown that nutritious mixtures of corn may be used with great advantage at a low cost. Their use and application should be guided by existing circumstances.

Animals should be selected as much as possible from an average class, character, and age; but an intelligent overlooker would soon be able to perceive, even among a mixed class where any differences existed, and modification is required.

Other Forms of Admixture.

Some would need a little more food than others —particularly aged ones—while there are others whose assimilative powers being more active, would derive more nutrition even from a little less food, and thus spare a trifle to their less endowed neighbours.

In the studs under the care of Mr. Hunting at South Hetton, Murton, Rhyhope, Trimdon Grange, Seaton Delaval, &c., &c., and Mr. Scott, in the old Hetton Collieries, animals of all ages are to be found, and, by the system carried out, are equally well provided for.

If, owing to the severity of the work, a more nutritious diet is called for, it will be found in the forms as follow, which provide it at an equally cheap rate.

Mixture No. 1 (*Low rates*).

		Weight. lbs.	Cost. £ s. d.
Peas	4 bushels . .	264	1 0 0
Barley	4 ,, . .	224	15 0
Oats	3 ,, . .	126	9 9
Bran*	. . . . . .	98	4 1
		712	£2 8 10

This mixture, divided among seven horses during one week, would allow each over $14\frac{1}{2}$ pounds per day, at a cost of 6s. $11\frac{3}{4}d.$, out of which 20·14 lbs. of N.M. (nutritious matter)

---

* The nitrogenous principle of bran is not calculated in these mixtures for reasons stated on page 83.

Other Forms of Admixture.

would be obtained. Divided among six horses each would cost 8s. 1½d., and obtain 23·63 lbs. of N.M.

Divided among five horses, each would cost 9s. 9d., and obtain 28·36 lbs. of N.M.

Mixture No. 2.

		Weight. lbs.	Cost. £ s. d.
Peas	4 bushels . .	264	1 0 0
Barley	4 ,, . .	224	15 0
Tares	1 ,, . .	67	5 4½
Oats	1 ,, . .	42	3 9
Bran	,, . .	98	4 1
		695	£2 8 2½

Divided among seven horses, each would receive over 99 lbs. per week, costing 6s. 10½d., and obtain 21·65 lbs. N.M.

Six horses would receive 115⅓ lbs. each, costing 8s., and obtain 25·26 lbs. N.M.

Five horses would receive 139 lbs. each, costing 9s. 7½d., and obtain 30·31 lbs. N.M.

Mixture No. 3.

		Weight. lbs.	Cost. £ s. d.
Peas	4 bushels . .	264	1 0 0
Barley	4 ,, . .	224	15 0
Tares	2 ,, . .	134	10 9
Bran	. . . . . .	98	4 1
		720	£2 9 10

Divided among seven horses, each would receive over 102 lbs. per week, costing 7s. 1¼d.; and obtain 23·86 lbs. N.M.

Six horses would receive 120 lbs., costing 8s. 3½d., and obtain 27·84 lbs. N.M.

Five horses would receive 124 lbs., costing 9s. 11½d., and obtain 33·40 lbs. N.M.

It must be borne in mind that good hay yields five per cent. of N.M. which must be added to the above for the quantity used.

It will also be observed that peas are named in the foregoing mixtures to the exclusion of beans. They are not so productive of constipation as beans, which on that account enables us to use them with greater freedom. Beans are, however, unobjectionable when used with oats and bran, chaff, &c., in sufficient quantities. Prices must regulate these mixtures from time to time, due consideration being paid to the N.M. contained in the various kinds of grain.

When the prices of grain are much increased, as they are at present, such mixtures as the following must be taken, and will be found adequate at an equally low cost.

From the *Field* of 21st September, 1867, we learn the prices current at Mark Lane were, for oats, 35s.; barley, 43s.; peas, 43s.; beans, 44s. per quarter of eight bushels, and tares, 7s. per bushel. Bran costs in Glasgow at the present time 6s. per cwt.

Other Forms of Admixture.

Mixture No. 4 (High rates).

		Weight. lbs.	Cost. £ s. d.
Peas	6 bushels	396	1 12 3
Beans	4 ,,	264	1 2 0
Tares	2 ,,	134	14 0
Barley	1 ,,	56	5 6
Bran	. . . . .	112	6 0
		962	£3 19 9

Divided among twelve horses, each would receive 80 lbs. per week, costing 6s. 7¾d., furnishing 21½ lbs. N.M.

Eleven horses would receive 87½ lbs. each, costing 7s. 3d., and obtain 23½ lbs. N.M.

Ten horses would receive 96 lbs. each, costing 7s. 11¾d., and obtain 25¾ lbs. N.M.

Nine horses would receive 106½ lbs., costing 8s. 9¼d., and obtain 28½ lbs. of N.M.

Eight horses would receive 120 lbs. each, costing 9s. 11½d., and obtain 32⅛ lbs. of N.M.

Mixture No. 5.

		Weight. lbs.	Cost. £ s. d.
Beans	4 bushels	264	1 2 0
Peas	4 ,,	264	1 1 6
Tares	2 ,,	134	14 0
Oats	1 ,,	42	4 4½
Bran	. . . . .	112	6 0
		816	£3 7 10½

Ten horses would each receive 81½ lbs., costing 6s. 9½d., and obtain 21 lbs. N.M.

Nine horses would each receive 90½ lbs., costing 7s. 6½d., and obtain 23½ lbs. of N.M.

Eight horses would each receive 102 lbs., costing 8s. 6d., and obtain 26½ lbs. of N.M.

Seven horses would each receive 106½ lbs., costing 9s. 8¼d., and obtain 30½ lbs. of N.M.

Mixture No. 6.

		Weight. lbs.	Cost. £ s. d.
Beans	4 bushels	264	1 2 0
Peas	4 ,,	264	1 1 6
Barley	3 ,,	168	0 16 1½
Tares	2 ,,	134	0 14 0
Bran		112	0 6 0
		942	£3 19 7½

Twelve horses would receive per week each, 78½ lbs., costing 6s. 7½d., and obtain 19¾ lbs. N.M.

Eleven horses would receive each 85¾ lbs., costing 7s. 2¾d., and obtain 21½ lbs. N.M.

Ten horses would receive each 94 lbs., costing 7s. 11½d., and obtain 23¾ lbs. N.M.

Nine horses would receive each 104 lbs., costing 8s. 9d., and obtain 26 lbs. N.M.

Eight horses would receive each 117¼ lbs., costing 9s. 11¾d., and obtain 29¼ lbs. of N.M.

Seven horses would receive each 134½ lbs., costing 11s. 4¼d., and obtain 33¾ lbs. of N.M.

Other Forms of Admixture.

Mixture No. 7.

		Weight. lbs.	Cost. £ s. d.
Beans	3 bushels	198	0 16 6
Peas	3 „	198	0 16 1½
Barley	1 „	56	0 5 6
Bran		84	0 3 9
		536	£2 1 10½

Eight horses would receive each 67 lbs. per week, costing 5s. 2½d., and obtain 16½ lbs. of N.M.

Seven horses would receive 76½ lbs., costing 5s. 11¾d., and obtain nearly 19 lbs. N.M.

Six horses would receive 89½ lbs., costing 6s. 11½d., and obtain 22 lbs. of N.M.

Five horses would receive 107 lbs., costing 8s. 4¼d., and obtain 26¼ lbs. of N.M.

Four horses would receive 134 lbs., costing 10s. 5½d., and obtain 33 lbs. of N.M.

Mixture No. 8.

		Weight. lbs.	Cost. £ s. d.
Beans	4 bushels	264	1 1 6
Peas	3 „	198	0 16 6
Barley	1 „	56	0 5 6
Bran		84	0 3 9
		602	£2 7 3

Eight horses would receive per week 75¼ lbs., costing 5s. 10¾d., and obtain 19¾ lbs. N.M.

Seven horses would receive 86 lbs., costing 6s. 9d., and obtain 21¾ lbs. N.M.

Six horses would receive 100 lbs., costing 7s. 10½d., and obtain 25½ lbs. of N.M.

Five horses would receive 120 lbs., costing 9s. 5¼d., and obtain 30½ lbs. of N.M.

From the foregoing arrangements and calculations, it will be observed there is an increase from ten to thirteen shillings per quarter in the price of grain and leguminous seeds, as charged in mixtures 1, 2, and 3, and those which follow point out the mode of combination which will secure the same quantity of N.M., or thereabouts, with only a fractional variation of cost.

The bulk will, however, be somewhat less, and requires to be made up by the use of hay, or hay and straw chaff.

As these mixtures are designed for hard-working animals only, it will be almost unnecessary after what has been said when speaking of animal heat, &c., to state that such food will prove pre-eminently injurious to idle animals, except given in very small quantities. To those doing no work or light exercise, oats are decidedly the safest article of diet.

Green Food.

Among hard-working horses, I have found the use of green food too indiscriminately adopted, and it frequently proves as injurious as a mass of cooked food.

That it is useful and beneficial I fully believe, but this occurs under proper management. When given, it should by no means take the place of corn. This is, however, too commonly done, the animal being allowed too much.

He then perspires freely, becomes weak and liable to disease. I have known for years that among town cart and cab horses to whom grass has been allowed as described, sore throats and influenza have appeared almost simultaneously with its use, besides colic, weed, &c., &c.

Two or three weeks' feeding while the plants are young may answer for easily wrought horses, but in my opinion that state of the animal's body which we term condition should not be so trifled with. Aptitude for work is not a condition which is obtained in a few days or hours. It is only obtained during weeks, and at considerable expense. Most persons know, or at least presume to know, what training the racer requires, and how long a hunter is in being got ready for the field; yet we find the same people sacrifice the condition of a draught horse during a season

H

when he requires the greatest strength, by the supply of an innutritious and watery food.

I maintain, if horses are in condition and required for work, that green food is an interruption to the formation and maintenance of muscle, and it should be avoided. If he requires rest, green food will be serviceable; and, like his more favoured master, he should be allowed a trip to the country, where, in a roomy loose box or covered yard, he can enjoy the green fruits of the earth, which are regularly mown and brought to him, protected from the rays of a scorching summer sun, or the pelting rains that fall, and flies which torment at this season.

When these conditions are not fulfilled, green food proves expensive and unprofitable. The animal loses condition and is below the standard for work, while he becomes peculiarly liable to disease, and exhibits the greatest difficulty in taking on flesh, appearing lean, hide bound, and generally betokening want of power and activity.

Similar remarks apply to the use of turnips or carrots. Moderately used raw in winter they prove serviceable—in excess they are positively injurious.

Economy of using Chaff and Bruised Corn.

With regard to the bruising of corn and cutting hay into chaff, I find the practice attended with good results. It suits a mixed class of animals better, and causes a more perfect mixture of each kind than would be derived from the food in the whole state.

It is an important proceeding where boys are employed; for where they have access to unbruised corn, they often take out beans, peas, or tares for pigs, rabbits, poultry, or pigeons at home.

The cutting of food, as already shown, causes a proper and continued flow of saliva—an important process, in order to ensure digestion of the numerous starchy elements of food upon which horses and cattle live. The cost* incurred is very little with proper machinery, and amply repays for the outlay in a very short time.

By the addition of *oat* or *wheat-straw*, a saving is not only effected, but the food is further aided in digestion. The usual proportions are one-fourth straw and three-fourths hay, but many persons use equal parts.

These are strictly non-nutritious agents as used. They are given purposely for providing

---

* It is frequently estimated that hay costs 2s. per ton cutting, and the bruising of corn one penny per bushel. Mr. Hunting, however, informs me that the work is performed at the South Hetton colliery for half these sums.

100 *Economy of Chaff and Bruised Corn.*

necessary bulk, and assisting in grinding down the other portions of food within the digestive organs. As an agent of nutrition hay is very expensive, and in that respect little superior to straw, which, with other food, I have known given regularly to animals, no hay being allowed, while the condition has been all that could be desired.

In all the cereals and leguminosæ ripeness of the plant is evidenced by the development and perfection of the seed in the various receptacles; prior to that stage the stem contains the nutrition. Notwithstanding this fact, so apparent as it must be to every farmer that the analogy exists in each, hay is allowed to stand for days, and even weeks, before being cut, when it must be an utter impossibility for any increase to take place. Growth is completed, the plant ripens, as indicated by the seeds becoming plump. They contain all the nutriment, and in the main are shed upon the ground by every wind that blows, leaving the hay nothing better than a fine sample of straw.

The higher price asked for this fine sample, we may infer, is to cover the loss occasioned by this species of neglect.

I wish it to be understood that I am not prejudiced to the exclusive use of cut hay and bruised corn. When given whole these substances may be effectively masticated, and the animals will appear excellent and pay well for the proper selection and mixture of food. I, nevertheless, consider that a larger profit accrues by *avoiding the waste* which always happens when hay is given whole (or long), besides suiting for general purposes much better.

Food so prepared will require *wide and deep mangers* fitted with cross bars, to prevent the animals throwing it out in their search for the more tasty portions.

On this subject many investigations have taken place at home and abroad, and the results are, without exception, favourable.

In France, Leblanc found that animals fed upon boiled food fattened, but lost vigour and became affected with disease; while dry food had a contrary effect. M. Charlier says, with cooked food the animals are very subject to disease, but since the regular adoption, by omnibus proprietors, of dry, bruised, and cut food, founder, colic, and illnesses generally, which each week were numerous, had become quite exceptional.

Pea and Bean Straw.

The question has frequently been put to me, " Is pea or bean-straw useful for feeding horses ?" To this an affirmative answer may be given, when the article has been carefully gathered and housed. It should always be cut up small, and mixed with the bruised mixtures of corn, and large quantities should be avoided by using with it cut hay. Equal parts of hay and pea-straw, or three parts of hay to one of bean-straw, will answer very well for working horses, but I deprecate filling the racks with either.

The many fatal cases of disease which occur from their use, is owing to the inferior condition of the straw, coupled with being in undue quantities and other irregularities, which too often exist in the farm stable.

Saving to be Effected.

Carefully carried out, these principles will effect an enormous saving, and I have no hesitation in stating that, among the numbers of animals employed in Glasgow and other large towns of Great Britain, it may be raised to *thousands of pounds annually*, and, in addition, a corresponding sum by the avoidance of disease.

The farmer need not grudge his horse corn, since it can be shown that he can be fed at less cost than many now incur on inferior hay, straw, and provender generally, and derive greater aptitude for work.

The poor man may also feed better and save a few shillings weekly, which would be well applied to the formation of a fund wherewith he could replace his animal in the event of death, without

Saving to be Effected. 103

resorting to the subscription system over his immediate district, which is too commonly done.

The principles are important to large owners, who might also raise a fund with the savings for the same purpose, and to remunerate, in some cases I could name, those who are able, and study to apply effectually the system calculated to bring about the change.

All food should be of the best quality and kind. If inferior kinds are purchased, and require disguising by some process to make them palatable, the sooner he who purchases such is removed the better.

No mixture or process of doctoring can render such available as nutritive food when the elements are not present, nor can any admixture of condimental nonsense effect it either. The experiments of Mr. J. B. Lawes have definitely proved that when animals improve their condition with the use of condiments—which in themselves have no nutrition scarcely—the result occurs from an *increased consumption of corn*. The proprietors of such compounds may state what they please in puffing their wares. But against their puffing it can be positively asserted, as an undoubted fact, that condiments, spicy foods, or by whatever term they are known, do not effect any improvement upon inferior food with which they may be mixed, and are not economical, as set against common salt, which is far superior at one-fortieth the price. On the other hand, they are expensive articles of diet, and can only be looked upon as substances quite dispensable, and of no great service in the feeding of animals.

Within a recent period a sample of food intended for working horses, cattle, and sheep, has been submitted to me by Messrs. Whyte and Cruikshank, Chryston Mills, near Glasgow, which, although bearing the name of a "Patent Prepared Food," it is only justice to state, partakes of none of the qualities of condimental or spicy foods. It is a preparation embodying, to a certain extent, the principles laid down in these pages, the whole of the ingredients being carefully selected, decorticated, ground, and baked. It is highly spoken of by several proprietors, and will doubtless prove a great boon to those who cannot devote attention to the selection of provender for horses, or where only one or two are kept. I, however, have no experience of its use, but judging from information received as to its composition, and the respectability of its inventors, have no doubt it will fulfil the ends claimed for it, and call for an extended trial.

Importance of Grooming.

There is one particular in the management of horses which so materially influences the effects of food upon the system, that it will not admit of being unnoticed, although the attention be exceedingly brief. This is *grooming*.

Importance of Grooming. 105

How far this principle is carried with many of our town dray and cab horses can be clearly ascertained by merely passing within a few yards as they stand in the street. After they have spent hours in the open air, the odour of the stable is strongly upon them.

There are, doubtless, good reasons to be assigned for this in some instances, the most common being that of absolute laziness. There are, however, cases where a groom or horsekeeper is expected to execute multifarious duties in addition to those of the stable, and in consequence the horse is neglected. Another fruitful source of neglect is to be found in low wages, and the mean endeavour to make up the deficiency by looking after per-centages.

Therefore it proves to his interest to be careless and incur expense upon all sides, which is done to an alarming pitch in some instances. A third cause is the unreasonable number of horses which are placed under the care of horsekeepers. This is a most monstrous practice in some of the coal mines. I have found it to occur invariably, that where the animals are working in the greatest amount of heat and dust—two or even three miles from the bottom of the shaft—where they perspire most freely, and endure every vicissitude inimical to general health, there they have had the least attention.

All this arose from an excess of duties.

In such cases I found men having the care of

almost a fabulous number of animals, and the only reasonable conclusion one can come to is, that such work and conditions are imposed upon the poor creatures, that it would amply repay the Society for the Prevention of Cruelty to Animals, and other adherents to Martin's Act, for an application to Parliament to institute special investigations into their condition, with a view to an amelioration. For less than one-twentieth —aye, one-hundredth—of the physical appearances of a pit animal witnessed in a horse in our streets, the keen eyes of the policeman would have a case, but from these places in the recesses of the earth there comes no cry, and nothing is known.

One horsekeeper had under his care fifteen horses and nineteen ponies; a second, four horses and twenty-four ponies; a third, twenty-three ponies; a fourth, two horses and thirty-eight ponies; a fifth, nine horses and twenty-eight ponies.

Three men had the care of five horses and eighty-nine ponies in a sixth instance, and three others had the care of twenty-two horses and fifty-one ponies.

These animals are to be fed, harnessed, and cleaned to go out to work at 5 a.m. by these men, who descend several hours previously in order to attempt an impossibility.

If we take the mean of these numbers, we shall find that each man had an average of thirty animals to attend to. The arrangements

Importance of Grooming. 107

of the stables are not always suited towards reducing the labours of the men, being frequently in a continuous line of stalls arranged on one side, which necessitates several journeys to each animal for turning to water, tying up, supplying with corn and hay when they cannot be fed at the head. Estimating the trouble which these men have, and the risk they run for a few shillings a week, one cannot be surprised that the horses and ponies do not receive their proper share of attention.

The idea of cleaning them is estimated as the boy did the operation of washing his hands and face when he refused on the score of their becoming as bad again shortly. Such an estimate, however, does not render the fact as it exists less flagrant.

Let each man be limited to a specified time for the execution of the various details expected from him, and it will be more apparent how absurd must be the belief that these animals can obtain one-fourth the necessary attention under their peculiar and extreme conditions.

Feeding with corn, each one minute	= 30 minutes.
„ hay, „	= 30 „
Harnessing, with repairs, two minutes	= 60 „
Turning to water and tying-up, one minute	= 30 „
Brushing down, each five minutes	= 150 „
Which occupies for thirty animals or five hours in all.	300 „

The men descend at 2 a.m., which only leaves *three hours* to perform a number of duties, the time for which, estimated as low as possible, is not sufficient to allow of their being effected in any other than a most slovenly manner—really occupies two hours more than the men can actually bestow on them. At night they are merely stripped, watered, and fed, in order to allow them rest.

To occupy more time with them would be also prejudicial, as the hours of rest would be materially interfered with; and consequently an average of thirty animals, estimated at about £300, are thought no more of than to value their care and management at the rate of fifteen shillings a week, or sixpence per head—the amount paid to the horsekeepers.

Here, where the truth of the old maxim, "A good cleaning is equal to a feed of corn," would be faithfully realized, it cannot be carried out.

When complaints were made, and exact conditions represented, all was pooh-pooh'd, and any alterations it was said would cost the estate £300 per annum, as ascertained by figures, which, emanating from the executive were reliable, but worth nothing when they arose from the mental calculations of one who was not a "Viewer."

Such is the connexion which exists between the skin and digestive organs, that if these poor

Importance of Grooming.

creatures could receive a guaranteed dressing of fifteen minutes only, each night and morning, the effects would be marvellous.

In a solitary instance, one man had fourteen animals under his care. As he was infirm and contented himself solely with the employment as horsekeeper, he could devote more attention to them than was possible in the other pits.

Every morning and night each was well dressed with a coarse brush, and left in a much more comfortable state.

His horses and ponies would have caused many owners of animals above ground to blush with shame at their superior condition and clean shining skins. They were always doing equal work with the animals of other collieries, but *suffered the least of all, and consumed the least corn.*

I have preferred to recite these facts rather than dictate a philosophical explanation of the uses of a brush and comb to the body of the horse. Those who are so pertinaciously obstinate as to deny him the influence of this luxury, I am afraid are not in a condition to explain the benefits of such an application from any experience of the adoption of similar means to themselves. However, these are considered to be measures not truly essential, and therefore, while the attempt is on the one hand to save, as these *pseudo savants* suppose, the sum of £300 per annum, they have not the philosophy to see, or the honesty to allow another to show, that four times that amount could be saved in the feeding in twelve months, and as much more in a variety of ways of which they cannot form any conception.

INDEX.

ABILITY, 48.
Absorption, 24.
Acids of digestion, 29.
Advantages of proper food and system, 42, 46.
Albumen, 30.
Albuminous principles of food, 28—30.
Albuminuria, 45.
Animal heat, 32.
,,   not maintained by fat alone, 35.
,,   produced in part from nitrogenous compounds, 32.
Animals hybernating, 35.
Assimilation, 24.
BEAN and pea-straw, 101.
Bran : its nature, uses, and abuses, 83.
,,   as a laxative, 84.
Breeding or pluck, 48.
Broken wind, how caused, 21.
Bruised corn, economy of, 99.
Boussingault and Papin, experiments to determine whether horses pass grain unchanged, 60.
Bulk or volume, 39.
CALCULI or stones in the intestines, 51.
,,   ,,   their origin, 51, 52.
,,   ,,   usual composition, 52.
,,   ,,   presented by Mr. Foreman, M.R.C.V.S., 54.
Capacity of large intestines, 26.
,,   small ditto, 24.
Care required in feeding after work, 60.
Carrots and turnips, 98.
Caseine, 30.
Chaff, economy of, 99.
Changes in chyme, 27.
Change of grain, objections to, 82.
Cheap food, what constitutes a, 81.
Cheeks, 14.
Choking, causes of, 19.
Chronic cough, one of the causes of, 22.
Chyle, 24.
Chyme, 27.
,,   changes in, 27.

Coal mines, feeding of horses and ponies in, 2, 79, 85.
,, neglect of horses and ponies, 77, 105.
Cæcum, 25.
,, principally contains fluid, 23.
Colon, 25.
Colliery estates, systems of feeding adopted upon, 74, 76, 79, 85.
Condiments, objections to, 103.
Consequences of imperfect system of feeding in coal mines, 2, 75, 76.
Cooked food, 18, 42, 101.
,, does not render food more digestible or nutritious, 41.
,, diseases arising from, 45, 101.
,, is expensive. 44.
,, injurious effects of, 18, 45, 101.
,, produces liability to disease, 45, 101.
,, not economical, 55.
Corn, mixture of, 89.
Cost of feeding horses in Sheffield, 72.
Cost of feeding upon oats, 65.
Cough, chronic, how caused, 22.
Cut food promotes salivation, 75.
DEVELOPMENT and maintenance, 8.
Deglutition, 17, 19.
Diabetes, 13, 42.
Digestion, organs of, 14, 108.
,, ,, should be in a healthy condition, 60.
,, acids of, 29.
,, in stomach, 22.
,, in intestines, 27.
,, rapid in horse, 22, 56.
Digestive process, 26.
Diseases arising from cooked food 45, 101.
Do horses masticate the whole of the grain? 56—60.
Dry food, objections to, 54.
Dung or fæces, 29.
Duodenum, 24.
ECONOMY of food, 71.
,, of using chaff and bruised corn, 99.
Effete or useless matter, 11, 29.
Elementary principles of food, 28.
Errors to be avoided, 40.
Essential characters of food, 29.
,, qualities of oats, 65.
Evil effects of insufficient food for young animals, 12.
Experiments of Boussingault and Papin, 60.
FALLACIOUS ideas as to the passage of unchanged grain, 56, 58, 60.
Fat or heat producers, 28, 32.
Feeding in coal mines, 79, 85.

Index. 113

Feeding, the manger system of, 55.
,, regular, 23, 46, 50.
,, saving effected in, by Mr. Hunting, 74.
,, system of, pursued at the Londonderry Collieries, 85.
,, ,, at the Hetton Colliery, 76.
,, saving effected by Mr. Scott at the Hetton Colliery, 80.
Fibrine, 30, 31.
Flesh formers, 28.
Fluids, passage of, 23.
Fæces or dung, 29.
Food, advantages of good, 12, 42, 46.
,, economy of, 71.
,, elementary principles of, 28, 29.
,, essential characters of, 29.
,, green, 97.
,, immediate object of, 8.
,, indigestible parts of, 29.
,, insufficient, effects of, on young animals, 12.
,, relative proportions of nutritious and starchy matter in, 63.
,, requires bulk or volume, 39.
,, steamed, objectionable, 87.
,, varieties of, 63.
,, when cooked expensive, innutritious, and not economical, 18, 42, 55, 101.
Foreman, Thos., M.R.C.V.S., collects specimens of calculi, 54.
Forms of mixture of grain, 89.
GASTRIC juice, 26.
,, digestion, 26.
Gluten, 30, 31.
Grain, economy of storing, 68.
,, objections to a change of, 62.
,, se'ection and purchase of, 68.
,, does it pass unacted upon? 57, 58, 60.
Green food, 97.
,, objections to, for hard-working animals, 97.
Grinders, 15.
Grooming, importance of, 104.
Gullet, 15.
HARD work, care required in feeding horses after, 23, 60.
Healthy condition of digestive organs necessary, 60.
Heat, animal, 32.
,, producers, 28—32.
,, ,, relative proportion of, in food, 63.
Heavy draught horses objectionable, 49.
Hetton Colliery system of feeding, 76.
Horse, digestive organs not intended for cooked or sloppy food, 41.

I

Hours of work of pit animals, 77.
Hunting, C., M.R.C.V.S., his determination of the proportion of husk in oats, 67.
   ,,   ,, his saving in the feeding at South Hetton, &c., &c., 74.
Husk in oats, proportion in different varieties of, 67.
Hybernating animals, 35.
IDENTITY of nitrogenous compounds from all sources, 31.
Ilium, 24.
Ill effects of maize, 70.
Immediate objects of food, 8.
Importance of grooming, 104.
   ,, of prevention, 4, 46.
Incisor teeth, 14.
Indian corn or maize, injurious effects of, 70.
Indigestible parts of food, 29.
Insalivation, 16.
Insufficient food, evil consequences of, in young animals, 12.
Intestines, stones or calculi in, 51.
   ,, their capacity, 26.
   ,, their division, 23.
Introduction, v.
Injurious effects of cooked food, 18, 45, 87, 101.
   ,, ,, insufficient food in young animals, 12.
JEJUNUM, 24.
LACTEALS, or absorbents, 24.
Large intestines, 25.
Large number of horses, importance of a superintendent for, 61.
Laxative, bran as a, 84.
Linseed, 71.
Londonderry collieries, system of feeding adopted at, 85.
Long fasts prejudicial, 23, 78.
Longevity promoted by good food, 46.
MAINTENANCE, 10.
Maize or Indian corn, injurious effects of, 70.
Manger system, 55.
Mastication, 15.
Mesenteric glands, 28.
Metamorphosis of tissue, 10, 11.
Mismanagement, mortality arising from, 5, 7, 13.
Mixtures of corn or grain for horses, 89.
Molar teeth or grinders, 15.
Mortality from mismanagement, 5, 7, 13.
Mortality saved by Mr. Hunting's system, 75.
   ,, ,, Mr. Scott, 81.
NATURE, uses, and abuses of bran, 83.
Neglect of grooming pit animals, 105.
Nitrogenous compounds, their identity from all sources, 30.

Nitrogenous principles of food, 30, 63.
Non-nitrogenous principles of food, 32.
,, ,, relative proportions in different kinds of food, 63.
OATS, 64.
,, cost of feeding upon, 65.
,, essential qualities of, 65.
,, straw, 99.
Objections to a change of grain, 83.
,, to green food, 97.
,, to the use of dry food, 54.
Organs of digestion, 14, 108.
Origin of calculi, 52.
Œsophagus, 15.
PATENT baked food, 104.
Pea and bean straw, 101.
Pharynx, 15.
Pit animals are much neglected, 77, 105.
,, their hours of work, 77.
,, horsekeepers have too many animals under their care, 105.
Pluck or breeding, 48.
Prehension, 14.
Prejudice against system in collieries, 4, 77, 87, 108.
Prevention, importance of, 4, 46.
Process of digestion, 26.
Profuse staling, 42.
Proportion of husk in different kinds of oats, 67.
Provision for maintaining warmth of the body, 35.
Ptyalin, 16.
RAPIDITY of digestion, 22.
Rectum, 25.
Regular feeding, 23, 46, 50.
Relative proportion of heat producers in different kinds of food, 63.
,, ,, of nutritious matter in different kinds of food, 31, 63.
SACCHARINE principles of food, 17, 28, 32, 63.
Saliva, 16.
,, is secreted abundantly, 17.
,, chemical action of, 17.
,, flow of, promoted by cut and dry food, 75, 99.
,, cannot be replaced by any artificial mode, 18.
,, quantity of, an important agent in digestion, 17, 99.
,, solvent action of, 16.
,, uses of, 17, 18.
Saving effected by Mr. C. Hunting, 74.
,, ,, by systematic feeding, 102.
Scott, Mr. L., his saving by feeding, 79.

Scott, Mr. L., his system of feeding, 79.
Selection and purchase of grain, 68.
Sheffield, cost of feeding horses in, 72.
Small intestines, 24.
Spicy foods or condiments, 103.
Staling profuse, 42.
Steamed food objectionable, 86.
Stomach of horse, ox, and man, 20.
  ,, small, 21.
  ,, of ox divided into four parts, 20.
Stones or calculi in intestines, 51.
 ,, ,, their origin, 52.
Storing of grain, 68.
Straw of beans, 101.
 ,, oats, 99.
 ,, peas, 101.
 ,, wheat, 99.
Strength or ability derived from food, 48.
 ,, required, not absolute weight, for moving loads, 49.
Superintendent, importance of a, 61.
Swallowing, 17, 19.
System of feeding in various collieries, 74.
 ,, ,, in the Londonderry collieries, 85.
 ,, ,, saving to be effected by a complete, 102.
TARES, 71.
Teeth, incisor, 14.
 ,, molar, 15.
Tissue, metamorphosis of, 10, 11.
Tongue, 14.
Turnips and carrots, 98.
UNDIGESTED food, 29.
  ,, grain, passage of, 57, 58, 60.
Urination, profuse, 42.
Useless or effete matters, 11.
Uses and abuses of bran, 83.
 ,, of dry food, objections to the, 54.
Uses of saccharine principles of food, 17, 28, 32.
 ,, saliva, 17.
Various forms of mixing grain, 89.
Varieties of food, 63.
WANT of condition, effects of a, 13, 97.
Waste of animal tissues, 10, 11.
Wasting of the body, causes of, 34.
What constitutes a cheap food, 81.
YOUNG animals require good food, 12.

THE END.

www.ingramcontent.com/pod-product-compliance
Lightning Source LLC
Chambersburg PA
CBHW020121170426
43199CB00009B/584